TESTIMONY TO LOVE

TESTIMONY TO LOVE

Gwen F. Steele-Perkins

With some commentary by Mary Tiffen

TIFFANIA BOOKS

First published as an ebook in 2016 by Amolibros,
http://www.amolibros.com
Loundshay Manor Cottage, Preston Bowyer, Nr Milverton, Somerset TA4 1QF

Published in paperback 2017 Tiffania Books
8 De Combe House, Crewkerne, TA18 7AH
www.tiffaniabooks.com

Distributed by Lightning Source worldwide

British Library Cataloguing in Publication Data
A catalogue record for this book is available from the British Library

ISBN 978-0-9570353-1-7

Typeset by Amolibros, Milverton, Somerset
This book production has been managed by Amolibros
www.amolibros.com
Printed and bound by Lightning Source

CONTENTS

Illustrations

BRIEF NOTE ON THE EDITOR, MARY TIFFEN

After studying history at Cambridge University, 1949-1952, Mary tried teaching, one of the few occupations offering equal pay to men and women in the 1950s. Temperamentally unsuited to it, she moved to a charity which paid very substantially less and then to an industrial company which eventually raised her back to the teaching level. In 1960 she met and married Brian Tiffen, who in 1962 joined the British Council. She followed her mother's example as the supportive wife on his overseas tours in Africa, Iraq and Europe, but, unlike her mother, could also accept paid employment in each place. When her husband took the early retirement on offer in 1984, this experience and the Ph.D. meanwhile taken led to an appointment as a Research Fellow at the Overseas Development Institute in London. For further details see www.drylandsresearch.org.uk. After retirement in 2002 she investigated her own family history, leading to a book, *Friends of Sir Robert Hart, Three Generations of Carrall Women in China*, 2012, which has been published in Chinese by the Guanxi Normal University Press in 2016.

The cover picture

My mother's sketch of her vision of God, which can be seen on page 45, was unsuited to a cover. This shows instead part of the illustration called 'Easter Cross and Brambles' courtesy of istockphoto, copyright: exxorian. It conveys the main features of my mother's vision, though there were no brambles where she stood.

Mary Tiffen

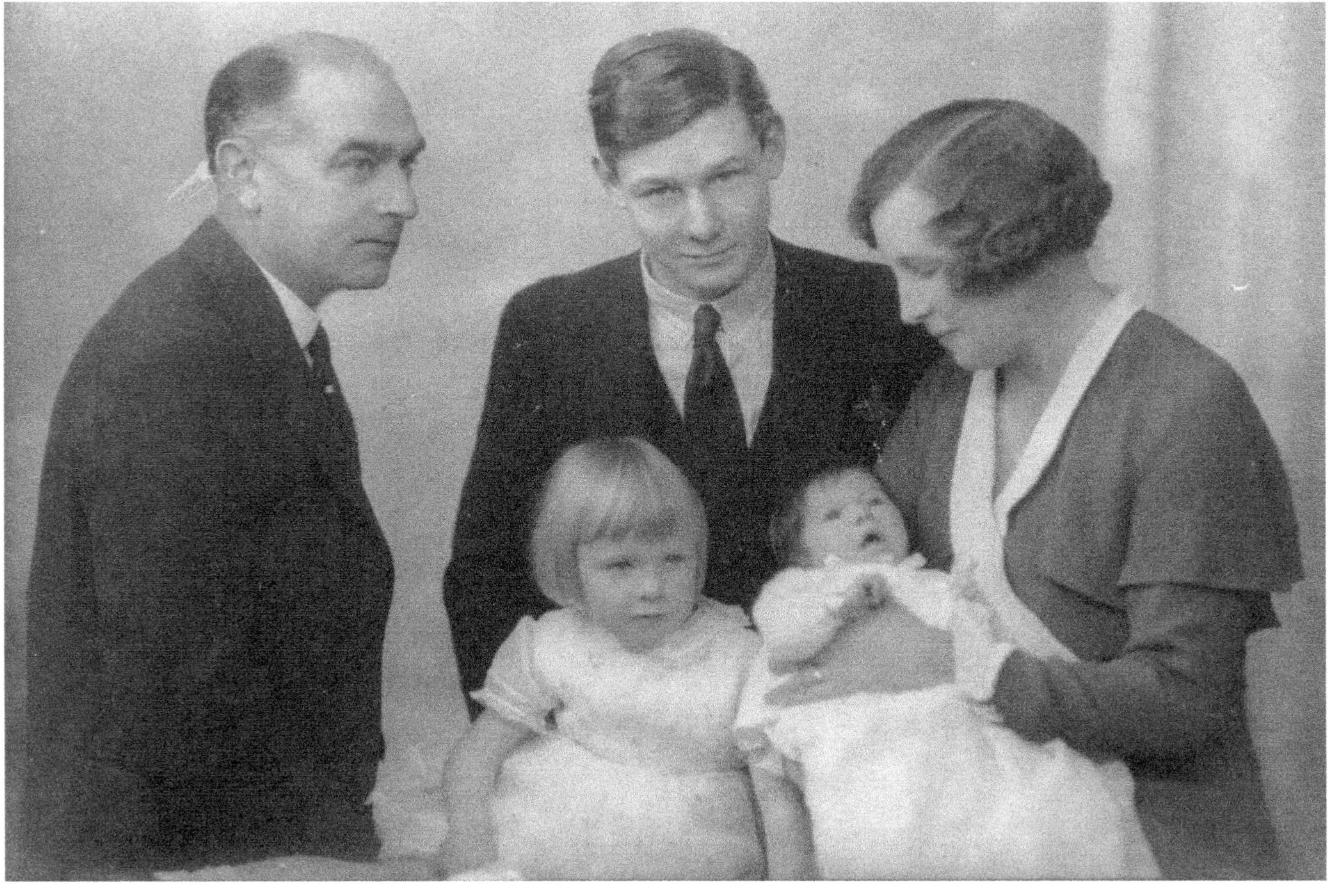

The complete family, Easter 1934, Horace, right, Gwen left, with John centre, behind his two young sisters, Mary and baby Susan

PREFACE

by Mary Tiffen

Daughter of Gwen Steele-Perkins

This book is a testimony to love: love of a woman for her man, of a mother for her son. But it is also testimony to a vision of God as Light and Love:

> You could not touch the Light, and yet you felt a wondrous Love from it.

This near-death vision came in May 1930, a year before I was born , after an operation to explore a septic miscarriage from which she nearly failed to recover. A final operation followed, aiming to end the possibility of more children. The Light had spoken of the afterlife but she was to return for another baby. She heard her mother speaking. There was also an impression of a death, which she took to be either hers or that of the baby to come. She scribbled notes on it immediately after she came round. She wrote it up while she was expecting me, thinking that she might die in childbirth. She completed it some months later, with an account of my birth in July 1931. This is reproduced in Part II. The death to come was not hers or mine, but that of her son John, at the age of eighteen, in March 1935. After that tragedy, she added the account of the events leading up to his death, which appears in Part III. She now understood her vision as foretelling his death but also enabling her to bear it by seeing death as a point of renewal and rebirth.

> Take heart and wonder not when a hardship happens if there is a God – rather believe as the writer of this book believes, that there is a purpose in all things, and when we have achieved

> the purpose for which we have been put on this earth we may, by our great desire to please Him, by our unselfish striving, be taken at the height of the earthly perfection of our soul to be made yet happier and more perfect in worlds to come.

What is now Part I, the story of her early life, was written in the 1950s. When she prepared the book for publication then, she put it in first place. I have kept it there, as it helps to explain the nature and experience of the woman who had this remarkable vision.

For her story is also a tragic love story. My mother loved my father deeply. As far as I can tell, theirs was a strong and physical love, although they did not share worries. This led to difficulties when they had financial problems. My mother was often very hard up on the sums which my father allowed her for house-keeping. His age and failure to get promotion obliged him to retire from the Royal Air Force in 1932. Soon he was responsible for not only a teenage son, but for me, born in 1931, and my sister, born in 1934. Even middle class budgets could be thrown by medical expenses caused by illness or births. Despite the Depression my father soon found work in Air Raid Precautions (ARP) first in the Home Office, then, in 1938, in Hong Kong, and in India 1941-5.

From my mother's account, he will seem hard and stingy but, as she herself said in a preface she wrote in the 1950s:

> Remember, too, when reading this, that it is the mother's, the wife's point of view. There are two sides of every picture – the father too had without doubt his worries, his trials, which would so overwhelm him that he could see no other point of view at the time. But all the time he loved his wife, her body and perhaps in his heart of hearts her character too – let's hope so. To give praise to others, to express his affection, he found hard. He very, very rarely could say tender things, express in words tender sentiment or sorrow – only write them. His feelings would overflow with anger, tears or cruel words, after having been, as I knew, through hell himself.

My father had been traumatised and changed by the death of his son in 1935, for which he blamed himself and rejected God. I myself know little of my father. I can remember him taking me for Sunday afternoon walks before we left England and family outings in Hong Kong at weekends. In June 1940 women and children were evacuated to Australia and we did not re-join my father till after his transfer to India in December 1941. In India he was only occasionally with us as his war duties meant he was constantly on tour. When the war against Japan ended in August 1945, he was sent to Burma to help with the repatriation of British civilians who had been interned by the Japanese. He formed a serious relationship with one of the internees, resulting in the birth of my half-brother Chris in 1947. He effectively left us in December 1945, when we returned to England and he to Burma. The consequent events are related in Part IV, first by my summary of my mother's account of the way she learnt in her fifties to earn a living. It finishes with my mother's own reflections on her life, the meaning of her vision, her change from submissive wife to independent entrepreneur and the inner conflict between love and fear that she experienced after her husband's return to Britain in December 1949. She was no longer the woman he had married:

> Until that great wrecker of …Victorian and Quaker upbringing burst on the world – the war [of 1914-18] – the writer of this book had never been out alone, unchaperoned, after the hour of sunset – not even to post a letter at the end of the street. Life in its hideousness and nakedness had been carefully screened, hidden and explained away. Life was good to the good, bad only to the bad. No path off the straight, flat, narrow way of silent obedience to the man in authority. For of course it had to be a man to rule the woman.

The love my mother had for my father, and the respect for a husband's wishes that had been instilled by her upbringing, meant that the love she had for her son was always sacrificed to enable her to be with her husband when he called. She came to realise that their son, John, had also frequently made sacrifices, underplaying his own suffering in order not to add to his parents' worries. She called later versions of her book "Sacrifice". I have retained this as the title of the third part.

My mother always wanted this book published. She kept initial drafts and letters that would authenticate her story. Some of these survived and are now with me, though others have become lost during my sister's and my various movements after her death. She wanted to share her vision, which she felt could comfort others. She wrote:

> I feel sure, so sure of my vision ... I did not see through the Light because it was so bright and overwhelming that I could see nothing else, but I felt like a blind man feels the living souls around me and heard their voices in the same tones as they used on earth. I did not understand clearly, as when I awoke to earth again it was so hard to remember every detail, but the gist is written here, blinded perhaps on purpose of that 'Love' to be recalled after my greatest sorrow, so as to comfort me again. Forewarned enough to make me strive to achieve my purpose because of my belief in the Light and the World to come. Comforted again by the Love afterwards by having my memory refreshed, and allowed to know that all was well with the one I loved on earth and failed to understand.

She showed me the first three parts of her book, ending at John's death, in the 1950s and asked me to help with publication. I was discouraging, partly because I rightly felt there was no commercial market. I also advised using false names for herself and her husband and putting the story into the third person to protect the privacy of living relatives and other actors. This she did but it reduced its impact. I have restored real names as those concerned have died, with the single exception of my half-brother Chris, who has agreed to be named. Parts II and III are the original 1930s' versions. She did not show me Part IV, written circa 1955-7, but it was amongst the papers I inherited. From it I summarise her achievements and growing independence after 1935 and the traumas caused by my father's return to England in 1949. I end Part IV with some recently found reflections jotted down 1959-60 on her life and the continuing reality in it of both her love for my father and the messages of her 1930 vision. This is her testimony to the Life and Love beyond death.

In this book anything in italic is by Mary Tiffen; all words in ordinary print are the words of my mother, Gwen.

PART ONE

PRELUDE

My mother's father was in the Chinese Imperial Customs, the upper echelon of which was staffed by foreigners. At the time my mother was born he was Commissioner of Customs in Chefoo, a port in north China now known as Yantai. (See Mary Tiffen, Friends of Sir Robert Hart: Three generations of Carrall women in China – www.tiffaniabooks.com)

Dawn in China

I was born in China in 1893, the sixth daughter and the seventh child of a family of nine. Five girls were followed by a son, four years older than me. Thus, my nearest sister was the eighth child, Phyllis, two years younger.

I am not sure from whom I obtained my religious teaching but, as I had no European nurse, it must have been from my parents. I loved my father, who was feared by most of the family, as a man of little patience. I remember going to church with him, and running to meet him on his return home from the office with my small sister. He was in his swing sedan chair, borne by four coolies. On some evenings the two small sisters would take him buttonholes of flowers. Once, I remember to my surprise being lifted on to his knee, and being told that I was the best of his seven daughters. This was all the more amazing as I had always thought of myself as the naughty one. My baby sister Phyllis was always loved, petted and forgiven, and my brother allowed to do whatever he wished, while I, forbidden to do likewise, was told, "You are only a girl, you see". How I hated that phrase; what wrath, what tears of passion it aroused.

The three younger children were left a great deal to the care of a Chinese Amah, who served the family for many years. My mother was preoccupied with her five elder girls, all of the adolescent age. There was a great deal of entertaining to be done, owing to my father's position, so my mother rarely had time to hear the younger children's prayers. That was left to the Amah who, though not a Christian, was a very upright conscientious woman. It was she who insisted on grace being said before meals and prayers being repeated out of bed, with folded hands, shut eyes and bended knees.

One day I refused to say my grace. Amah insisted. "Why, Amah, you make me? You no believe in my God." "Kunghan (Miss)," the Chinese woman answered, "everyone believes in a God. Even a wild man feels he must worship something. We know inside us there must be a God. You must worship according to your mother's custom, I, to my mother's teaching. How do we know if it may not be to the same God, worshipped in different customs? My Mother told me God like one Sun – plenty rays – if I be good I go up my rays – you, yours. What is good for the Chinaman to eat makes the English man sick, so our customs are best for our natures, yours for yours. Do as your Mother teaches, and say your grace. I, too, give thanks before I eat. It is a good custom to say 'Thank you'."

I was greatly impressed, obeyed, and never forgot her teaching. The sudden realisation 'There is a God. Even the wild man feels that within him he must worship something' set me thinking. I began to watch nature, and to wonder at the miracles of God displayed in nature. I enquired more about God from my Mother. Sunday evening readings of "Peep of Day" commenced just before bedtime. My mother sat with us two small girls on bentwood chairs on either side. These readings were interrupted by the birth of a second son. This brought me still closer to Phyllis, for Amah's time was taken up with the new baby. We got a new nurse, whom we disliked.

In 1902, the whole family went down with scarlet fever, excepting my mother and baby brother. *[Her elder brother also escaped it.]* I had it first, Phyllis next, then my father. These two died, and my grief and desolation was great. I was left with no one to play with, no parent to call me, even when I was naughty, "the best of the bunch". I wandered, like a lost soul, in the garden, and cried at night in my solitude till Amah heard me.

"Our mothers teach us there is no death. Don't cry, little one. Your sister lives with your father on the other side. He would be lonely without her. You loved him. Let him have one of his large family for companionship in his new life. He lives, she lives. They can see, hear and understand our writing. Comfort yourself, little one. You will go one day to join them. You ask your mother. It is the custom of everyone who believes in a God, to know that God lives, and has another world, and we too will live in it after this life, if we do well."

Next morning I went to my mother's room and made enquiries about this after life, and found Amah's and my mother's custom was to believe in a God, in prayer and in an afterlife. I took heart, and prayed to that God with all my might to give me faith and knowledge that my sister was safe and happy with Him. I took Amah's advice, and wrote a letter to my sister, and posted it in a hole in the wall at the back of the kitchen. We had always used this as a letter box. Next day I went again, full of hope. There were two letters: one, mine to my sister, and underneath it, a letter in my small sister's writing. It had evidently been written to me while I was ill, and before my sister fell a victim to the infection. It spoke of her loneliness, and her hope that I would come out and play with her again. Some drawings and flowers ended the letter. I was overjoyed. Though I realised it had been written before death, it seemed an answer to my prayer, as I had not found it the day before. It now served a purpose, for it showed me God had heard the cry of a child. I ran to my mother and to Amah, crying with tears of joy.

"She is happy for she has written. She lives. There is indeed a God and an afterlife". My mother took the little letter and put it in her prayer-book. And Amah said: "And now, Little Miss, you write to your sister in your secret code (their code) and put it with some flowers in her grave, the same one where she is with her father."

I ran out into the garden, and gathered a bunch of mauve clinging wisteria, the flowers both children loved. We had called them 'dropping tears' flowers, for they grew like grapes or tears. I made them into a bunch, and tied on my coded reply of thanks to my sister. With joy in my heart, I went with my mother to the cemetery. I was carried in the same swing chair my father had used, my mother leading the way in her own basket chair. That night I prayed: "Oh, God, do please help me to believe in you, and that Phyllis lives with You. Be kind to me, and let my flowers live and not mind the hot sun and then I will be sure about You and Phyllis. Please, God, do this for me."

The heat wave broke. The rainy season started, and when I was again taken to the cemetery, the flowers, my flowers, were still alive. Now I was certain – no doubt left. Shortly afterwards, the family packed up, and went home to England, where they were taken in by a good-hearted bachelor uncle, my mother's brother. What matter that the grave was left behind? Phyllis and Father lived – all was well.

School

I was still lonely. My other sisters were much older than me, the next older sister having died shortly after reaching England of appendicitis. The teasing elder brother went to a boarding school. The baby brother, aged just two, was much too young to be a companion. I felt lost, and so was sent to a day school. There I was not quite understood. No one seemed to either want my love or sense my loneliness. When about eleven, it was decided that I had better be sent to a girls' boarding school. Here I flourished. My House Mistress was a woman of great understanding and sympathy; one who encouraged confidences. As I had spoken Pidgin English during most of my childhood, I found it very difficult to master the English language, much to the amusement of my school-fellows. My spelling, too, was hopeless. I was given extra lessons by my House Mistress, both in reading, writing and spelling. As a result, I became acquainted with the best in prose, verse and with the spiritual. I also believed in prayer and its power. She took me to London to hear a lecture on "The Way to Pray" which left a great impression on my youthful mind. I was confirmed soon after. I did well at the school and became Head of my House for the last two years of my school life.

She attended Winchester High School, 1907-11 (now St. Swithun's). Her older sister Kath had preceded her, 1905-07, working for her Higher School Certificate and a teaching qualification. Girls were prepared for examinations and university entrance if they wished. My mother had two years in the sixth form, but, like most, did not take the 'stressful' examinations –regarded as unnecessary unless a girl really needed to earn her own living. A letter she drafted in 1911 to her housemistress shows she felt that a girl did need to be able to earn her own living, even if her fate was to be a housewife and parent, because the need might arise. (Her own father had died at fifty-two, leaving his wife and children initially very poorly off). She said she would like to be a writer, but realised her spelling was a handicap. Her music mistress thought she could be a singer, but her mother would not permit her to go on stage. (She told me later that she had been able to earn the odd guinea by singing at private parties.) She had ruled out teaching as she lacked patience, but later showed she could have done it.

The war and marriage

For me, the war suddenly broke upon the world. In 1914 I had gone to Germany for three months to visit cousins, and had been treated with great friendliness by girls of my own age. I landed in England on Friday, and war was declared on Monday.

Like my contemporaries, I longed to do my share but my mother was reluctant to let me go. However, I studied at the Red Cross and Home Nursing Classes, and passed my examinations. I was sent to nurse *[as a V.A.D., Voluntary Aid Detachment]* in Exeter, many miles from my Quaker family. I was still ignorant of sex. Mine was still a world of platonic friendships. My reading had always been carefully chosen for me and I had never been allowed to read the daily papers. "Not for young ladies," my Victorian mother would say. My innocence protected me. I failed to take in the meanings of vulgar remarks, and the ordinary "Tommy", ever a gentleman, soon realised he must not say things unfit for my ears. "Hush, here's Nurse," would be remarked on my entrance. The men laughed and chatted with me, in big brother fashion. I enjoyed nursing.

I was billeted on nice people, a retired doctor and his wife. I had spent a year with them when Horace, their only unmarried son, twenty-eight years of age, serving in the Navy, returned on Christmas leave, [December 1915]. I had had a tiring day. The hospital was crowded with wounded and operations had been in full swing. My apron was soiled with clearing up. Feeling too poor with the expenses of Christmas time, I had not bothered to change to a clean one, but had covered it up with my winter coat. My hat, a large brimmed straw uniform one, was drenched with the rain, and hung in a limp whirl round my face. I meant to steal straight up to bed but as I tip-toed up the stairs the parents called me in to meet their son. They had purposely left the sitting-room door open to catch me. I went back down, saw a good-looking man about town, chatted lightly while feeling my worst, and retired to bed after ten minutes.

Next morning I crept downstairs for work at a quarter to six. As I was unbolting the front door I was called from the smoking room. "Nurse Carrall, I have some tea here for you." I went in, and saw a splendid fellow, immaculately dressed, dark lounge suit and spats. "Good gracious," I exclaimed, "what are you doing up so early?" "Oh," he replied, "I always like to see the sun rise." This was not very credible on a damp cold winter's morning but I thanked him. He asked if he could come with me to the hospital. "Oh, no, I'm afraid not," I replied hastily. "The men will be hanging their heads out of the windows, and will greet me with that song, 'and who were you with last night?'" "Well," he pleaded, "let me come as far as the corner of the hospital road." To this I agreed.

We chattered of other Christmases and home life, and parted good friends. I promised to spend my two hours' off duty with him. Somehow I already felt that he was going to mean something to me, although I rather feared him. He pleaded for my company; I asked for a chaperone. Every moment of my spare time he fought for. He begged his people to come to his aid, which they did, arranging theatre parties and motor trips, and inviting me to the family Christmas party. I was allowed to bring my own nurse friends, girls as young as myself, for chaperone. They were attractive too, I hoped more than myself. For I still feared this man. He was so ardent, so insistent for my time and attention, so different to the usual type of sick and ailing men with whom I was surrounded.

On Boxing Day the Hospital gave an "At Home". I was to take part in a play, with some of the other nurses, and my host and hostess and their son had been invited. I had had the day off to prepare for night duty. When the play was over, I found that the Doctor (my host) had obtained leave of absence for me on the plea that, if I were acting all the afternoon, I could hardly be expected to nurse all night. So they took me home with them. The young wooer had engineered another surprise. I was to go out to a pantomime with him, one of his sisters acting as chaperone. After the show was over the young couple took the obliging sister to her home, and then walked leisurely back to the house. It was a beautiful cool starlit night. He took my arm, saying, "It's rather frosty, you may slip." I smiled, and let it rest in his. On reaching home we found a note in the hall from the old people, "Hot milk and whisky in the morning-room." As I sipped my hot milk, he took a gulp of whisky and popped the question: Before I could get over the suddenness of it all, he kissed me. "Now, won't you answer me?" he pleaded. "Tomorrow," I said, and coyly left for bed with yet another kiss from him.

I slept well, too tired to think. Next morning I was awakened by the maid with the early tea, and instructions to stay in bed for breakfast. I thought, "This will give me time to think what I am going to say to that very determined young man." But I was not given the chance. I heard the ardent young man come out of the breakfast-room, saying "Mother, Gwen and I are engaged." I shuddered in bed, and blushed red. I heard my future mother-in-law's excited shriek as she passed the news on to her husband.

I had felt from our first meeting that I had met my fate, but love, as I had imagined it, had not enveloped me in flame. "Well, well," I comforted myself, "perhaps love is a flower, and I am in the early bud stage." It was soon developed by this kind family. His mother insisted that as soon as I was dressed, I should be shown by my fiancé a drawer full of ladies' portraits. They were signed "Yours affectionately" or "With love". My fiancé picked up each photo in turn, saying: "This one I met in Shanghai," "And this in Sydney", etc. I smiled and handed the photos back. Then I gave an inward chuckle as I saw two photos picked up at once, but only one was shown to me, the other sat upon. I waited till the drawer was empty, and then said: "And who is the one you are sitting on?" "A girl I was once engaged to, but I broke it off." "Oh, well," I said, "I too have suffered that, so we start even." I kissed him and we went downstairs to burn the whole lot.

The old man was obviously so very glad to have me as a daughter-in-law. He kissed me and warned me that life would not be easy. "I fear my baby boy is the black sheep of the family. He has no idea of money, if he wants a thing he will get it. He bought a car the other day without asking me and put it down to my account. I was never so angry. He is in debt now. You will have to wait, but you may steady him. I hope you will be married from our house, as one of my daughters, my dear, and I should like to give you away." I embraced him warmly and thanked him.

How happy I became, overflowing with joy. I was granted three days' leave to take him home to see my mother and ask her consent before he had to return to his ship. As we went up to London he begged for an early and quick marriage. "For how else can I see you? You could not come to me and how could I get more leave? It has taken me one and a half years to get this." But my mother was not so pleased. I was the last daughter to be married. There was no need for haste, she averred. He had only £180 a year, and debts. How were they to live? Better to be engaged, and wait till the end of the war.

On Wednesday, Horace had to see his heart specialist, for he had developed an extraordinary heartbeat, and it was for this reason that his Christmas leave had been prolonged. He came back from the interview, depressed. The specialist would not say that he would agree to the marriage unless he saw the bride-to-be. "Well, let's go and see the man tomorrow," I said, "and do a theatre afterwards." An appointment was made. We were both nervous. He went in first, leaving me alone, and then both the specialist and fiancé came out. The great man looked at me and I felt like a piece of furniture. Then he said: "A great strong, sensible-looking lass. She will see you through. Marry her. It will be the steadiest thing for you. A good anchor." "Oh, Doctor, am I as bad as all that?" I exclaimed. We all laughed. The Doctor shook me warmly by the hand and, when I asked about the heart, he said: "It is a nervous heart. Make him like milk better than whisky. It may go on for years and outlive you. If it gets too upset it may go off at any moment. Keep him calm. But then you may be leaving me now and be killed at the street corner. How can one tell? Anyway, it won't affect the next generation."

Horace returned to his ship and I to my nursing. He returned in February, determined to be married. I obtained another three days leave, and we went up to town, and told my mother. She at last reluctantly said that if his father agreed, she would. It was then Friday. We did a theatre in London, and went down to the father on Saturday. Horace bought an excellent bottle of port. "It will square the old man," he told me. And it did. I heard him on the phone, sending a telegram to my mother, before the men joined the ladies upstairs. "Come down Monday. Married Tuesday."

On Sunday we visited the Bishop for a special licence. Horace's father obtained permission for me to marry in my nurse's uniform, and the bridegroom was in his naval one. A young army doctor acted as best man, and my greatest girlfriend, also a nurse, attended me. His mother invited some of the other nurses to be present, and some of the men came in their hospital blue.

My mother came down early on Monday, and we went to the draper's to buy the barest necessities for the trousseau, all in cotton, Quaker fashion. The old vicar, who had christened the bridegroom, agreed to marry us. I squeezed my groom's arm, when he referred to me in his address as a bride 'in my virginal white'. A great Red Cross adorned my apron, and my uniform was blue. ...The bridal party returned to the house to be photographed, and then I changed into my usual Sunday frock and away we drove – hearts high, full of hope. He had had engraved on the inside of my wedding ring "Omnia Vincit Amor".

We were to spend the night in town. Having lunched in the train, and both feeling keyed up, we decided to run down to the old home to see my sisters who were not able to come to the wedding. *The house in Kingston on Thames, where my mother and her sisters lived with her brother, their Uncle Jack, remained a place of refuge for the girls during marriage crises or necessary separations.* After tea, we went back to London, the shops being still open. As we walked up Regent Street, he saw a lace and crepe-de-chine nightie. "Have you one of those?" he asked. "No," I replied, "mine are all cotton". "You must have it," and he gave me the money to purchase it with. When the shops closed we looked for lodgings. He suggested the "Strand Palace". "You stay in the taxi, and I will see if there is a room." He went in and asked for a room for himself and wife, but was told there were none. "But I have brought my bride," he pleaded. He came back to her. "They want to see you." My shining nose, as I used no make-up, passed inspection, and we obtained a room. *My mother said her mother had felt quite unable to tell her the facts of life, and after the wedding simply said to my father, "Be gentle with her; she knows nothing." Despite his rushed wooing, my father obviously succeeded in this and clearly made my mother happy in their sexual relations.*

The next day we went by train to the Birkenhead docks. The first room we got was dreadful. I had never thought it possible to sleep in such a slum, for which we had to pay twenty-eight shillings a week. After two days I hinted I would like a change if I could know how much he could afford. I found a clean house, and a kind stout motherly old soul, with a sick husband and a large family. Here we stayed for six weeks, until his ship sailed, and then I had to return to my mother.

It was in these poor but happy surroundings that we decided that if anything happened in the war to the man I now so greatly loved, I should at least have a living remembrance of him. We used to peep into other people's prams, and quietly give each other a squeeze. "How do babies come?" I asked. "Can't you guess?" he queried. "No," I replied, "you see you promised we would not have any when we married. What will the parents say?" He laughed at my anxiety. "Oh, they really don't expect us to keep that promise, you know." "Well. How do babies come?" I asked again, as we sat on the shiny black hair cloth sofa in the front parlour. "Whisper to me how you think." I whispered. He laughed, and laughed and laughed, rolling on the floor, and laughed again and again. "I'll tell you tonight. You really are a child. Did not your mother tell you?" "No," I said. "She said you would know. And you promised not to have any. My mother won't discuss things like that, you know. It is not genteel."

John, our firstborn, was given to us on 1 December 1916, nine months and nine days after our wedding day. The nine months of waiting were very trying. My husband was away, his letters irregular. He wrote pages and pages, telling me what he desired his son to be, and then he would say he wished for a daughter. Then again he would change his mind after having read of a good boy's character. He sent me a book, heavily underlined where I was to read, and he decided to choose my reading. Curiously the hero of this book died at an early age – still a youth. So I read his choice of books, and sewed dozens of baby's tiny garments right up to all that a child would need until a year old. People told me it would bring me bad luck to look ahead so far, but I laughed at them, and prayed, believing that my man would be kept safe throughout the war.

I was back with my mother. A sister was at home with her three year old daughter, suffering from a bad nervous break-down following the birth and from the unhappiness of her married life. I took charge of the toddler while my mother cared for my sister. I hid my feelings at the wretchedness of my sister, hoping that if I was brave and strong my child would inherit bravery and also be strong to control his feelings. I wrote long letters to my husband and he answered them by loving assurances that all would be well in time. He too showed such trust in God that I was able to play my part better.

The battle of Jutland came. I read of it in the morning's paper at breakfast. My husband's ship [the Campania] had sunk. I could not touch a morsel. "Think of your baby," said my mother, "save him for remembrance sake." I prayed "Not my man, oh God, not my man." I went upstairs to make the beds, and attend to the toddler, praying as I worked. A telegram arrived… I tore it open. "I am safe – all is well. Love, Horace." I rushed to my mother, put the telegram in her hands, and fled upstairs to thank God and weep.

We had a weekend's leave and went to see his people. Afterwards he returned to his ship, I to my mother. Again at the end of November Horace was home. The joy of seeing him again gave me false labour pains, so we decided to move to London, to be nearer the nursing home.

John was born on 1 December 1916 ... I had a difficult birth, and had to have stitches afterwards. I was kept in the nursing home for three weeks. I was tired, and the babe would not suck and lost weight. Once home I abandoned the four hourly feeding regime the home had insisted on and fed him the natural way of every two hours, rising by degrees till he became so strong that he was taking four hourly feeds at six months. I was proud, and wrote "Nothing else but his mother," on his photo. But as a consequence of one of the stitches going septic I had to have three operations, one six weeks after the birth, the second five months, and the third seven months afterwards. This was the most expensive, as I had to engage a nurse for baby until I had recovered and took sole charge of my baby son again.

I lived the unsettled life of a naval officer's wife, travelling to join my husband as soon as ever he was at a suitable port. The baby travelled on a pillow strapped to the luggage rack of a third class carriage. In early 1918 I received unexpected news. "Have been asked to start at the new Air Ministry. Shall I?" I wired back, "Yes, we will be together."

Young married life

So we started real married life, not just spasmodic 'honeymoons'. The first task was to get a nurse for John, now eighteen months old, but very jealous of Daddy. He used to cry piteously if he saw me embraced, which annoyed his father. Putting baby's crib in the dressing-room seemed only further to agitate him, and if he heard the voice of the strange man to whom his mother gave so much attention, he would yell loudly, "My Mum, my Mum." As my husband had to go daily, including Saturdays, up to town, he hardly had the chance to make friends with his son. It was difficult for me, with one of my two disappointed that the baby preferred the mother, and the other feeling displaced. We decided we must have a nurse for the baby, so I could to give more time to my husband. *[The first nurse was a disaster but a nurse-housemaid more successful.]* The boy went back to sleeping in his parents' room. He recovered, and learned to love his father. Their friendship grew. They would go for walks, the father telling the lad fairy stories and tales of animals, especially one about a monkey.

I was worried at the small lad always being alone, and so he was sent for two hours daily to a small kindergarten. He only had two terms when we again moved. John was no sooner being settled at one school than he had to attend another.

From the Air Ministry we were moved to Aboukir in Egypt. John loved Egypt, unaffected by the boiling heat in which he would lie stretched out on the burning sand, in only a shirt and shorts, and a sun helmet shading head and eyes. He loved to escape with the old native watchman, to drink tea with the Arabs in their tents and partake of the Eastern bread. He never suffered any harm, although it worried me. I started home lessons with him but they did not go very well. I could not keep his interest long, and decided he needed companionship. So I started a little school for officers' children to which eventually twenty-two children came. At first it was free, each bringing his or her own equipment. But as the school grew, a governess became necessary instead of voluntary help, and a small fee was charged. I worked regularly every morning and tried to introduce the best discipline. The Commanding Officer gave a hut near the church for the school house, with a veranda. Here the pupils would gather at 9.00 am and march into church for prayers. Afterwards work would go on from 9.00 am to noon, when prayers ended it. A tea-party and prize-giving ended the term. John did not profit much as I kept him in my class, owing to the gossip of the other officers' wives that I was making a profit. The auditing of the accounts showed a loss resulting from the salary of the governess. John did not learn to read but in other respects, such as in losing his shyness with others of his own age and being able to hold his own against them, the lessons learned were invaluable. Further, it kept the children in the cool and quiet instead of on the hot beaches and in the Arab village.

In the cool of the afternoon there were bathing parties and picnics. One day the G.O.C. called on us, but we happened to be out. But John was in, and the G.O.C. was so struck with the lad that the two became the greatest of friends. He told us how, when he drove up in state with his outriders and his equerry behind, the small lad, muddy and dirty with his play, went down to meet them, and asked them to come in, apologising for the absence of his parents and offering him a drink. The kindly General thanked the lad, but refused the drink. "Well, have some tea," said John. This was again refused, but the lad was so pressing that they came in and sat down in the veranda. The General was delighted with his little host. After this, the General used to call on his way to bathe, and take the lad with his party. He told John he had his own train and a red carpet was laid down for him and his wife at Cairo station. "I wish my Mummy and Daddy could have all that." "So they shall," replied the G.O.C. – "my wife hates the hot summers and your mother can take her place – I'll send the train to fetch you and lay down the red carpet at Cairo station."

He kept his promise! The General invited the whole family several times to Cairo to see the sights, and took them up the Nile in his launch. John loved the museums and relics of the Pharaohs the best, which the General felt to be unnatural in so young a boy. But our quarters were built over some ruins, and John and his father used to search for old coins, vases, and relics of the time of Cleopatra. The Bible stories read to him by his mother were a stimulant, and his surroundings made him realise the truth of the Scripture history. But he was not without spirit.

One day, having just recovered from tummy trouble, he was left at home whilst his parents played tennis, and he had been told not to eat any fruit. Normally, he was allowed to help himself to the grapes on the sideboard. On returning home, I saw a small heap of grape stones and skins left to show me that grapes had been eaten. "John," I called, "have you eaten these when we told you not to? "Yes" he replied. His father thereupon punished him and sent him to bed. Next morning all the remaining grapes had been eaten. Pips and skins had been left to be seen. "Horace," I said, "look at these." "John," called his father, in a fierce voice. "Yes, Dad," was the reply, equally fierce. "Come here." He came and took up the same attitude as his father; feet apart, hands behind his back. "Did you eat the grapes?" thundered the father, knitting his shaggy eyebrows and looking his fiercest. "Yes, Dad," replied the lad, in a perfect imitation of his father's voice, face and attitude. I had difficulty in restraining a smile. "But I thought I gave you a caning for it." "Yes, Dad, but I thought it was worth it," answered the lad with perfect respect. "Don't do it again. We trust you, my lad. I punished you, not for eating the grapes which your mother told you not to as you were not well, but because you had broken your trust to us. I like to feel I can trust my boy."

And he never failed again.

John and his faithful dog, Rip, used to be invited to parties on their own, as my afternoons were given to entertaining friends, or playing golf or tennis with my husband and other members of the Club. I never worried much about John, as long as I knew Rip was with him. Both dog and boy loved the sea, both swimming out together, Rip keeping beside his young master.

England and school for John

From the joys and freedom of Egypt we returned to England, and Rip had to go into quarantine. Now began a new era for John. He had been free – free to play, free to go about alone, and go out to any meal with friends. He had been trusted, believed, respected, and had only once taken advantage of this trust and freedom. Now he was to be sent to boarding-school, amongst boys alone, and to become one of the herd. … He could not even hear from me without a stranger reading my letter and his answer, as he could not yet read, although he could draw and paint and use his hands really well. He knew history, scriptures, geography well, and was able to draw from memory, and in detail, maps of various places, putting in spots for towns, and mountains and rivers. But reading was his great stumbling block. He had no idea of sound or music, and could not even march in time. I begged that he might be sent to a home-like school first, but his father felt that he had been long enough among girls, and sent him to a school recommended by one of my sisters. … We knew nothing about it, and a new Head was about to replace the one my sister knew. …

We were staying in a small furnished flat near my mother. John loved his 'Granny' very dearly. At a child's party at her house Granny said to me when I came to fetch him: "Something is wrong with your boy. He plays as hard as he can and then suddenly lies on the floor, too exhausted to play anymore." I found him lying on the floor by the fire. "What's wrong, John? Tired?" "I have a bit of a sore throat, and I don't feel like playing, that's all." *[John had diphtheria and was ill for three months, during which time my mother nursed him, in isolation, with her mother or her husband shopping for her when she put out a list.]* He was able to go for walks with me but had to be quiet for fear that his heart might be affected. At last by April he was strong enough to have his tonsils removed. …

John was a keen gardener. His father had brought home from Egypt some scarlet flowering creeper seeds. John begged for some seeds and was able to grow plants where his parents failed. "How did you do it, John?" "I thought of the Nile mud which these plants love so much. So I paddled in the dirtiest water of the canal, and filled a pail, mixed it with a little sand, and manure, so as not to have the soil too wet, as Egypt is a dry country." They grew in the sun all the summer long.

He went to a local school for the rest of the term and had extra reading lessons. But his teacher found his attention everywhere but on the subject at hand. So his father decided to send him to the boarding-school in Sussex. He said the boy needed discipline. I had perforce to agree. As he had had no opportunity hitherto to play games, he had not learned to use a bat or ball, or had any football practice, another reason for a boys' boarding-school. He now had to wear long trousers and an Eton collar, a contrast to shorts with shirt sleeves. Though now nearly nine he had still not mastered reading.

My husband's C.O. motored us down to the school. I had to fight hard during the journey to keep back my tears. On arrival we were taken in to meet the Head and his wife who showed us round the school. Then John came out to see us off. He kissed me, saying quietly, as he pressed my hand: "I will be all right, Mother." He waved his hand as we drove off, then turned and walked back alone. My husband's C.O exclaimed: "By George, what control that lad has, what pluck. My boys wept – yours behaved like a man. He should go a long way, that boy of yours."

That night I could not sleep. I lay wondering whether all was well with John, and for weeks afterwards kept on waking up and thinking of him, so that my husband chided me. He refused to go to see the boy. "It will only upset you both," he said. "If he could write and read," said I. "These copy-book letters of his are all dictated."

The Christmas holidays came at last. I went up to town alone to meet him at Waterloo. A crowd of small boys all alike in long trousers tumbled pell-mell out of the train, but I could not see the fat smiling baby face I knew. Suddenly a boy who had been standing opposite me said, in a disappointed voice: "Mother, don't you recognise me?" "John," I said, surprised, "my darling!" As I greeted him I hastily added "You have grown into such a man, I was still looking for a baby boy!"

And I laughed to comfort him, but my heart wept with dismay that I had failed to recognise my son. His face had altered so much with suffering that it was now drawn. During those holidays he spoke little of his life at school, but his table manners had deteriorated, and we understood from casual remarks how much he disliked it. We, however, put it down to natural home-sickness. His father told him all men had to go to school, and described the rough time he had himself undergone. The end of the holidays came, and I saw him off at Waterloo. Both I and he had tears in our eyes ... so I hastily kissed him and handed him over to the master in charge without waiting for the departure of the train.

Again my husband refused to go down during the term, not even at half term. "Sports will be at the end of the term. We will go then"

They went. "How are you, John?" "Oh, all right." We talked as he showed us over the school – his bed, his desk, etc. Never once did he let us see his misery. We had to leave him to go into tea. After tea we caught him off guard. I was horrified by his face, such hopeless despair and misery. He had been standing near the matron, who had let him realise his failures in the sports which he, so anxious to please the parents he loved, already felt too keenly. His father too was astonished, and ran up to the lad. "What's up, John?" he asked. The smiling mask took charge again. "Nothing, Dad. I will be home soon, won't I?" "Yes, dear. Only two more days."

I wept on the journey home, and for long into the night. And John?

During that term Rip, the dog, returned from quarantine. My parents had moved out of the boarding house into a small unfurnished thatched cottage belonging to the new R.A.F. headquarters. The rent was low, but it had only three rooms, and a small scullery, no gas or power. My mother made a start to buy furniture, and make a home, feeling this was necessary while her husband was still in the RAF and money was good.

The cottage was surrounded with beautiful woods, which had been sold to be cut down. Rip hated to see the trees felled. One day a woodsman came to fell a pine tree on the border of our garden, and Rip would have none of it. One beautiful morning, the dog was let out for his early morning run alone, while we dressed. In the midst of breakfast we looked at each other, both hit by a feeling that something was wrong. "Where is Rip?" We got up – breakfast half-eaten, and went out to the back door. There the dear dog stood, looking pitifully up at them, as if to say, "I am finished". He could not move or make a sound. We carried him into the sitting-room and laid him, with his head on my knee, by the fire. My husband went at once in the car for a vet but it was too late. The dog was buried undisturbed in the small garden under a pine tree.

His grave was made into a beautiful garden by John and me, when the lad returned for his holidays.

Neither I nor John ever loved another dog so much. My husband brought others home, but they never stayed long. Rip's memory stayed so fresh that when John was eighteen, and had to write an essay for one of his examinations on "A Faithful Friend," he wrote of his dog. He wrote so well that he passed with honours in English, a subject he had found so difficult in childhood. We were surprised. But John gave as his reason for passing, "The dog seemed to be with me the whole time, still a helpful and faithful friend."

During the holidays both parents were astonished at the boy's exceedingly bad table manners. He bolted his food, and crowded his mouth with large uncut pieces. On being reproved he said: "That's how you have to eat at school. Matron insists and does it herself. It's always 'Hurry up, John', or you are made to feel an ass in front of all the other chaps."

Asked how he liked the school, he always said: "Oh. I suppose it's all right," in front of his father or any friend, but to his mother, he would drop little hints of his dislike, and despair of ever succeeding there, saying: "It's awful never being able to be alone – there are always crowds. Even if I go upstairs to my bedroom, that loud-voiced woman (the Matron) will shout at me as if I was deaf. She never trusts me, Mummy. I know she hates me, and I hate her. Some days I do things on purpose to make her furious; I feel I have won then."

Towards the end of the holidays he could not bear me out of his sight. Once or twice I had found he had wept himself to sleep. His pillows and sheets were quite damp, but he never asked to remain at home. He had been told by his father that every boy had to stick it, and so he was going to try to do so too. His school report was bad. His work we expected to be backward, but his conduct was so very different to his normal attitude at home. He owned he behaved badly on purpose to get out of Matron's clutches. He had found that a form of punishment was garden work, just the thing he loved. "You see," he explained – "You could get away from crowds then, and be with the sergeant. I understand soldiers, and airmen, and they don't nag like women. I like this sergeant too. He's a friend, and very decent."

About ten days before the school was to commence again John's tummy became completely upset. It seemed as if he had severe dysentery. He would weep at night so much so that we put his bed in our room. The local doctor could not understand it … A specialist was consulted, who chatted with the lad alone. He said it was a nervous complaint, owing to suppression of feelings. There was no doubt the boy hated and loathed his school – he must be removed. He advised a local school. The school did not take day boys, and so it was arranged for John to be a boarder, but allowed home once a week after church service: and if there was a cricket or football match the parents were invited to take tea and look on. On being told that he was not going back to the old school, but to this new one in the same village, he recovered at once, as if a miracle had happened …

John liked his new head master exceedingly, and his matron, and the school atmosphere. It was home. The dormitories only had three or four beds. *The whole place was well-furnished*. The boys were expected to behave as gentlemen and treat things with respect. And they did. He was really happy there. He used to bring a friend or two to lunch and tea on Sundays. His work he found very difficult still, especially his reading and dictation. *It is possible that John suffered slight dyslexia, which would not have been recognised at the time. My mother had some difficulty with spelling, as did my sister.*

A year after he had been at this school, when he was just beginning to feel on his feet, his father was appointed abroad to China, in the Fleet Air Arm *[October 1928]*. But he failed to pass the medical examination for Foreign Service. This was very worrying, for he was due to retire in three years' time and the Treasury, then very hard pressed, urged for his retirement at once, which would mean the loss of his full pension. I persuaded him to go to a London specialist, and the R.A.F. sent him to another specialist. These disagreed as to his fitness. My husband saw the Chief, who happened to know him well, and who ruled that he had better "D … well go and die." So to China he went. I was most anxious to go with him, but my husband knew his son thought much of Christmas, and as it was now late October, he advised me to stay for the Christmas holidays, and sail in January.

There was a great deal to do as he had only been given three weeks' notice, and more than half this time had been taken up seeing doctors. I was left to get rid of the house, pay bills and generally clear up. I saw my husband off, and then went to the bank where we had a joint account, and found to my added worry that he had been allowed to overdraw for two months as he was going so far afield. He, knowing I was going to stay with my mother, thought to himself, "Oh, well, she will be all right."

I was not, I was dreadfully worried, so worried that friends had to come to my rescue. I had no sooner cleared things up, as best as I was able, and gone over to my mother's, when a cable arrived, dated 23 November, from Singapore. "Come. See Air Ministry re passage." I was greatly distressed and worried. Had the heat proved too much after all? What could I do? A sister lived near, and ... offered to take John for the holidays, as we both realised that our poor old mother had more than enough to cope with, with an out of work married son and his daughter on her hands already – and with no cook or help of any kind. I also thought the influence of my sister's husband, who at this time was away ... might be good for John, who was to lose his father just when he was greatly in need of a man's point of view. So I gladly accepted. I explained my financial difficulties, and it was agreed that I should give a banker's order for £5 per month, making it sixty pounds for three holidays. Then I visited the Air Ministry but ... was told that as my husband was joining the Fleet Air Arm, he had no station, and so I was not entitled to a passage, which my husband had not realised. So I visited every shipping agent to find the cheapest and quickest route. I found the Army had a trooper leaving Port Said in fourteen days. Knowing the Air Marshall in Egypt I asked the Ministry to wire him, to book a passage for me. I also decided to see if a rich friend would agree to take a post-dated cheque for fifty pounds.

I went to see John, showed him the wire, and said: "What am I to do?" "That's all right, Mother," was the extraordinary reply from this boy of barely eleven years old. "You must go out to him. I know what married people are." I could have dropped down with surprise at his calmness, and matter of fact answer. I explained that by taking a train across France and catching a boat at Marseilles I could just be in time for the trooper ... "Well," said the lad, "if you are leaving tomorrow, take me out for supper tonight." I then explained I had to see my friends and get a cheque out of them, and sell the car before I could go. "Come on, then," said John. "But sell the car first. Best take it to the garage that has looked after it and knows it."

I was very pleased to get thirty-five pounds; fifteen pounds cash and a receipt for the unpaid bill. We next called at the rich friend's house and were asked to supper. After supper, feeling fortified by good wine,

I asked for the loan of fifty pounds, in return for a cheque dated for the day of my arrival in China. This was kindly given. Back to school we went, by now nine o'clock. *[They said their goodbyes.]* No tears. I turned away, glad there was no car to drive as my eyes would keep filling, blink as hard as I could. *[Government services in my own time abroad paid for two annual holiday trips for children. It was not so then, and arranging holidays with friends and relatives also on tight budgets was difficult.]*

Next morning I was seen off by the sister who was going to care for John, and by my mother who came to town with her. We stopped to cash my fifteen pound cheque for my car at the local grocer's, so as to leave with my sister five pounds for John's December holidays, promising to see she had the next payment on 1 January. In town my mother and I cashed the £50 cheque. I parted with £32 for the train and boat to Port Said, and £3 to my mother for my late odd expenses ... and to buy a Christmas present for John. I paid the taxi driver handsomely and caught the boat train as it was about to leave. As I looked out of the window my mother looked so worn, shrunken and transparently pale that I felt a sudden fear that this might be the last time I would see her on earth. And, indeed, so it was.

Those winter holidays were John's most miserable ones, as he told me only when I returned home. ... My sister's husband was very much annoyed when he found he had John for the holidays and, John said, was rude and unkind. He certainly wrote very unjust letters to me about the way I had dropped the boy on his household, which were very upsetting to us as well as to John. ... I did not blame my sister, knowing how trying husbands can be, especially when they consider a wife's life and a house is theirs and theirs alone instead of shared. Half way through these holidays John was sent back to his tired and worn granny. I received little letters like these: "They (the aunt, uncle and niece) have all gone out to the Pantomime, and so I am writing at Gran's. I have not been to anything these holidays, but I do like the Park. It is dull without you, but I am glad you are happy with Dad. Ever your loving son, John." And again: "It's nearly the end of the holidays – I am glad. I am staying with Gran now. Please arrange about my next holidays properly. Uncle says you never arranged for me, but I know it is a mistake. ... I have never wanted school so much."

Before the next holidays arrived two tragic losses were to occur for John. His dear old head master became very ill and died before the end of the term. Half way through the term he heard his Gran had died suddenly from a stroke. He was more than ever determined not to go back to his uncle's, so he arranged to stay with a school-fellow as a paying guest. We had met his mother and sister on Sports Day. John wrote: "I expect you remember Jim. He has said I can go to his home for next holidays at two and a half guineas a week. I hope that's not too much for you. I do so want to go. In fact I arranged it in case you had not time to fix me up." The mother of the school-fellow also wrote to me and so it was fixed. *[These holidays went very well.]* Unfortunately John went down with very severe measles after these holidays. ... We had to pay an extra fee for special nursing, and the new Head wrote towards the end of the term: "John still seems unable to pick up. His heart is a slow, tired one. We have him out of doors as much as possible, and I am afraid he has missed a good deal of this term's work."

My husband arranged to send the lad to a widowed sister of his, as a paying guest. She had a house by the sea, so he went there and, much to John's annoyance but to his good, she fussed over him. Nevertheless, in spite of looking well, as the school reported, he became ill with German measles, and was again pulled down and kept back in his studies. For the winter holidays he went to Cornwall to stay with a sister and a niece of his father's mother. He enjoyed these holidays, and was made to feel wanted ... Easter term came again, and with it 'flu and a cough. The Head's wife wrote advising sending John back to the aunt he had thought too 'fussy', writing: "He looked so well after those holidays and must have been stronger for, in spite of the German measles, he picked up and did a good term's work." So back he went for half his holidays, spending the other half at the sea with his old grandfather and grandma, my husband's parents. John liked his grandfather and found his discipline like that of his own father. "Grandpa is like Dad," he said with a smile. Before the summer holidays came again, I fell ill in Hong Kong.

PART II

REVELATION

My mother's original hospital notes on her vision have disappeared, as explained in the preface, though a manuscript of her speech survives. There are some scraps of what she wrote up, often in pencil, while expecting me. She made one or more copies in ink in an exercise book to send to her witnesses for their comments. This 'manuscript book', as I have called it, was finished on June 27th 1931. She refers to it as her first book. The doctors asked her not to use their names for reasons of medical etiquette. (Dr. Moss may have also requested the deletion of an account of a ticking off he gave her, which reappears here using a 1950s' version). As they are long dead, I have restored names. She used the same manuscript book to start again on September 16th 1931 with an account of my birth and early life. Enlarged and amended, it became a typed book in the autumn of 1932, probably with the aid of her sister Kathleen, whose typewriter I think I recognise. This second book, as she called it, with slight rearrangements to make it more chronological, is the basis of this section.

Hong Kong (1929)

On my arrival at Hong Kong I found the life of a round of gaiety amongst people one did not know rather forced and tedious; the mornings were especially long and boring for we were staying at the Peninsular Hotel, Kowloon, and except for bringing a few flowers to arrange in my bed-sitting room there was no other work to do. Ladies would call on you to wander through the shops or drink coffee at some hotel or other, the men were all at work, the golf course was too far away to get out to and be back for lunch, as well as being too expensive to keep on paying for two lunches, one at the hotel and one at the golf course.

We had no private means, only our pay, and so we had to be rather careful. I found that by wandering round the shops you were always spending the odd sous, which, after all, mount up in a surprising way, so I called on the Bishop and asked him if there was any work that I could do in the mornings while my man was away. He asked me if I had ever taught. [*She told him about the school in Aboukir.]* The Bishop was delighted and insisted there and then on phoning up the Headmistress of St. Stephen's College for Chinese girls, a Church Missionary Society school considered the college for higher class girls and spoken of as the Girton for Hong Kong. It was arranged for me to teach English throughout the school; Hygiene, Roman History and Geography to the senior classes; singing, writing, dictation and simple arithmetic to the younger children and babies. I found it hard work but very amusing and entertaining. The classes consisted of 22-30 children. I am afraid I did not keep very good order amongst the boys and girls ageing from 7 to 12 years, but the babies and older girls were most delightful to teach; the others were very highly spirited and mischievous but very amusing. They wrote beautifully, a perfect copy book, and would criticise my writing on the board; but I soon overcame that difficulty by making the best writers write for me on the board and then, of course, they all wished for a turn. One small boy wrote and spelt perfectly so I patted him on the back and said "Excellent." "Say it in Chinese," he said. I replied that I could not speak Cantonese, only a little Northern Chinese. He said something, which I repeated and all the class immediately made long noses. "What are you doing?" I asked. "You said 'Make a long nose' in Chinese," was the reply. I fear I laughed and refrained from learning more Chinese.

The older girls of 14 to 18 were most anxious to learn and very polite and sweet to teach. ... I set them essays to write on "What is your religion?" (They were not all Christians, in fact very few.) "What should a nation's ideal be?" and "Women's influence on a nation". I lectured first, expressing my ideas on these subjects and reading and quoting from various famous people their ideas; then I asked them not to repeat what I had said but to think for themselves. The results were excellent and gave me much food for thought, such as if we were right in allowing ignorant persons to go out as missionaries amongst a class of such high thinking people with such high ideals as these girls had. They quoted their ideals as taught by Confucius and Buddhism and also another man whose mother had taken great care of his moral training when a lad, even to moving house rather than that he should play with bad playmates in the street.

I taught in the morning until my husband had to go north to Wei-Hai-Wei with his ship, and then, needless to say, I went too. When we returned to Hong Kong my husband did not wish me to continue teaching, as he felt that brother officers and others thought I was being paid, whereas really I had to pay out 1 dollar 40 cents to get to the school and back. As luck would have it the school was well staffed now that the mistress, whose place I had taken, had returned from leave in England.

The Bishop, hearing I was back, wrote to me and asked me to attend some religious meetings organised by a Mrs Foster. I refused. I said I had a belief of my own which was not as orthodox as the Church might wish – it was my belief, however, which I had formed after having lived through the War, during which I was a nurse and saw much suffering – and that I might give offence to the older ladies of Hong Kong who had not been through such upheavals as those war days were. Nevertheless the Bishop asked his wife to write to me and to send me the book this meeting was studying and discussing every Tuesday fortnight for an hour, from 11 a.m. to 12. I am afraid I did not agree with the book; it was full of much reading and theory but you felt the man was a learned person with very little experience of the hard hits of life – you could picture him sitting writing in the comfort of a quiet study, surrounded by books he approved of, in a quiet well-ordered country vicarage. You did not feel he had had any experience of real temptation, any human understanding those experiences give one. If you met him you would expect rather a pious monkish man, what we lay people would call "fearfully orthodox". So I called on the Bishop and told him I felt I would only upset things; the Bishop said he did not mind, he still wished me to go. "Give me more active work," I said, but all he could give me was the organizing and buying of 2,780 Christmas presents for poor Chinese, mostly C.M.S children, and to attend a needlework morning at which ladies came in and made all kinds of Chinese garments, bandages, etc., needed for the various C.M.S hospitals and maternity wards. I was made Hon. Treasurer of the Hong Kong Branch and had to collect the funds as well as to see to the buying and packing, etc. I also agreed with the Bishop that it would not hurt me to go and listen to one of these religious meetings at which only women were allowed to attend – no padres, not even a bishop.

The lecture

So one Tuesday morning at the end of November I went up to the Cathedral Hall and introduced myself to Mrs. Foster who was expecting me. She, in turn, introduced me to one or two of the other ladies; I did not know any of them, most of them were older than I was. We all gathered round some small tables that had been linked together. Mrs. Foster sat at the head and opened the meeting with a prayer. Then she began her address. I am sure the author of the book we were discussing would never have recognised her version of his meaning. I was astonished, then annoyed, then disgusted and finally comforted my feelings by realizing we had been promised a discussion at her conclusion. But the gist of what she said was something after this style: She described Christ as a poor beggar and she even wondered if He was clean. She said He desired to even the world, to do away with luxury, etc., such as cars, paintings, and various arts and to make all men equal both in position and wealth. She thought herself it would help the world greatly if we took by force the wealth of the rich man and forced people to do without all enjoyments, arts, music and other things which she described as merely luxury. She even quoted some Russian philosopher which she had lately read. After speaking for an hour and ten minutes she ended by saying: "I am sure you will all agree with me, in fact I can see no argument against to discuss."

There was silence; no one spoke but sat like sheep. I felt I could not sit still; if I did I would be agreeing, and everything in me shouted 'No'. So I arose and said: "I am sorry, I do not agree with a word you have said." One may imagine the shocked silence my statement caused. I felt the very air bristle – I, a newcomer, among these elderly and learned ladies. Mrs. Foster replied, "I presume after such a statement you will give your reasons." "Yes, certainly," was my answer, "but I can hardly do so now as you have left us no time for discussion; we have husbands and some of us homes to look after and you have spoken already ten minutes over time." "Will you give us your views at the next meeting?" "Certainly," I answered, and with that the meeting adjourned.

Needless to say I felt very perturbed at what I had undertaken, for I was not used to speeches and addressing people, especially on a subject like this. I felt my husband's position too. He was acting as the Senior Air Force Officer of a new Service out there and we were a mere handful among a swarm of Navy and Army people.

However, I spent some time in silent and earnest prayer asking for truth and guidance and the real translation of God's meaning to be shown unto me. I borrowed a small New Testament from the Dean's Vestry, for I possessed no Bible, and read the Gospels – St. Matthew and St. Luke; more particularly the latter, he being an educated man – and compared notes of these two testaments with St. John's and St. Mark's. Then I wrote in the morning while my husband was away the following: –

> In our last Meeting, Tuesday 10th December, we were more or less told that the height of God's perfection on earth could not be until we were prepared not only to give up all our worldly goods but to <u>take by force</u> from others their properties and wealth and divide all this, giving to each man an equal share. It was thought that by this violent method we could get brotherly and spiritual love, as there would no longer be envy for another's goods and comforts. By spending no money on developing these luxuries we would have more to keep for ourselves as a community. The word "spiritual" was not mentioned, only "brotherly love", but it is in the background for we are gathered together to work for a spiritual, godly love throughout the world: to mould ourselves like Him, and to do His pleasure.
>
> Now in these few sheets, which can be tremendously enlarged upon, I am trying to prove that to take by force is the wrong starting point, the wrong way to reach God's likeness and to be able to commune with Him freely, which is our aim in life here on earth, and through the ages to come. That Jesus never recommended violent methods, although, of course, He did lose His temper now and then, such as when He cleansed His Father's house of the buyers and sellers, and also when He cursed the fig tree; still it was only to punish, and the very fact that He was so human gives us more hope for the future. That He was born to the educated class of the people of His day, and that He enjoyed, and helped to create luxuries which, after all, give ultimately a higher perspective of life. His life, I wish to prove, shows but one thing, the power and glory of the Spirit, which has to be given freely before it can rise to the height of feeling, seeing and working its power. Each man giving himself. No amount of forcing will give an individual of any temperament the desire to give freely of himself, and until we do that we cannot hope to commune with and feel God. My point is: do not try to drag down to a lower level

those to whom God has given the power to soar, but rather try and educate gradually the lower natures up, so that in the next world they may become nearer to God's likeness, even if they failed in this. We cannot hope to be like God at once: it will take ages of perfecting ourselves, but, nevertheless, because of Jesus Christ we know that there is this Spirit, or Holy Ghost, through which we may commune, not only with Him – God – but He with us, and we with other souls both here on earth and still living in the onward worlds, through which we ultimately will pass. It connects us, and will always keep us in one great community, no matter where we be.

God, as the Creator, the King, the Father, has the choice, the power to inspire or conceive His Spirit in anyone: in other words, to give birth to His Spirit in anyone He wishes. Now, being a Father, the model and aim of mankind, one feels and is told in many places that He can give that Spirit to any one of us, and so, naturally, He has more than one child – not one, but many sons. There is hope for us all to be His children: I don't say we are, but we see many who are, and I feel strongly that where we British fail is to think only of Jesus as the only possible son, instead of the best and most powerful yet produced, who was sent to us for our dense eyes to open and see the working of the Will, Communion or spirit of God – or rather, shall we say, of the hope and power of God in man. Other sons have been felt, and felt very strongly, by other nations: Mahomet, Confucius, etc., etc. As you see, I call all good men of high and God-like ideals, who have left a mark on the world, sons of God. We have been drilled to think of Jesus in certain ways which, if we had picked up the New Testament and read it as a book without any other point of view pressed on us, excepting the fact that we had travelled East, we would think of Him differently, and it is in the light of how I picture and think of Jesus, and the work which God wishes us to do through Jesus' example, that I am going to describe to you.

I wish you to realise first that this is my point of view, my opinion after a fairly trying and active knocking about by life. So no one need feel hurt if they do not agree, but if it is of any use or comfort to anyone to know that to me it has proved very true, I am only too delighted to have cheered them on the road to victory.

Now what is this Spirit, the first knowledge of which we see in Jesus and hear of its powers from Him? Surely it has to do with "will", our own effort and belief in ourselves – the power of feeling thought, or rather the power of feeling the consciousness of the Holy Ghost. For that Spirit is the Holy Ghost, or pathway to connection with God. The power of feeling the caress of that Spirit, which really is the caress of God, as the Spirit or Holy Ghost is the pitch of vibration on ourselves when we have had a touch or clear communication with God. To analyse that caress: I have felt it very like a human one, only of a greater power of duration. This explains the need of feeling and creation in the form that it is so as to develop us up to the power of feeling God's love.

We see in life many forms of both development and underdevelopment: the well-built man but brainless: the man with brains and a small body: the dwarf – the genius. We also know the organs of the body differ in size in various people – so we get the man with the liver, the men or women who are over-developed in their organs of creation, and hence their difficulty of control is greater than ours. Jesus, we are told by St Luke, was a perfect boy, and developed into a perfect man, both physically and mentally, and, as we know, spiritually. St Luke II. 52: "Jesus increased in wisdom and stature and in favour with God and man." The stature we are born with, and every nation now is making an effort to perfect it by exercises, etc. etc., in schools and places of commerce and business, so that we will ultimately be perfectly built people. The wisdom and favour of God we have to study and learn and prepare for, as He did; therefore, there is hope for us once we have learnt to have the will or belief to start.

I have spoken of the feeling of the Spirit and the power of development so that when we go step by step over Jesus' creation, life and death, we will see why He inspires us and gives us hope as a man and as a carpenter. The greatest inspiration is that we can all be the same if only we have faith, if not in this world, in those to come.

I am just going to show you my picture of Jesus and Mary, His Mother, so as to let you see life is not so hopeless, and does not need such fearful upheavals, as was suggested in our last meeting, to even all things; but what is needed is to find this Spirit and be able to use it as we can switch on or off our wireless sets.

God appeared to Mary the Mother of Jesus, who was already betrothed to Joseph as a fairly rich and inspiring man. You can imagine, from her description, which you will find in St. Luke that she saw a well-dressed person, with command of an assured person of good breeding – so wonderful that he must be a prince or angel. Her fright over what had happened to her, and her flight to Elizabeth, her friend and cousin, makes one feel it was not Joseph. Hence it gives one a reason to believe it was the communication of the Spirit of God which conceived. Not such a miracle after all, once we possess the power of etherised wave communications, which God is now beginning to show us is possible by allowing us to see through science the power of wireless, which after all is only the first, and a little step, to greater things. Yet by it we dense people can see how miracles are worked. Who of our great-grandmothers would have believed? Why not, therefore, believe through the Spirit and mutual linking of the Holy Ghost that this thing did happen (as we feel when we dream, and our husbands have been away from us that they have been with us. Surely it is only another step, after all, to conceive). Elizabeth's and Mary's conversation also points to it not being Joseph, and their power of expressing themselves either shows that they were educated women or had had an inspiration of the Holy Ghost, which can 'make all men speak in their own tongues and be understood by all', such as at Pentecost. A thing which, by-the-bye, we are gradually developing, and which will unite us all more than anything else to God, that is a common language, education and understanding. St Luke was a doctor, and evidently to both these women as he writes: "It seems good to me, also having perfect understanding of all things from the very first, that thou mightiest know the certainty of those things wherein thou has been instructed." I think we may take for certainty from the way Mary fled to Elizabeth that it was the first time; that she was very frightened, and surely if it had been Joseph she would have stayed with her own people and married him straight away: but you see, she was only 'betrothed', and out East they are, too, very strict about these things. The marriage ceremony alone shows a woman must be at least thought a virgin. We can imagine peace being restored to the engaged couple owing to this great inspiration of the birth of a Son of God, and so Mary and Joseph continued wending their way together.

Now Joseph was a carpenter, a man of property and wealth. All shopkeepers out East are looked up to – men of count. A carpenter, in those days especially, was a man catering for the wealthy, for the comforts and luxuries of mankind – a respected man – has a house, tools and a shop. Joseph must have been a man of wealth and property, otherwise why bother to go to be taxed? He had to make a long journey with a woman 'great with child', and evidently very near her time as the baby was born before they could find a resting place – and such a child as they hoped – the Son of God. If they had been poor they would have been contented with the tents which are still to be found surrounding the villages; but no, they looked for comfort as people who were used to it. So they went to an inn, and only as the inn was full and birth commenced did she seek the manger. You can imagine the excitement and the need for haste. A stable is a place in the East shared not only by animals but humans, as those who have travelled know, so not very dreadful. It was not England or English people: the natural thing to those people would be to point out the stables, nice clean straw for the poor woman in her first agony. Think, too, of the narrow streets of Eastern towns, full of curious people: of course she had to go somewhere and quickly too. Again the inspiration given by God to the wise men was not to look for a beggar but a prince, or at least a well-to-do person. Hence rich gifts, and to find Him they looked amongst the well-to-do, otherwise how did Herod hear of Him and order the slaughter of all the male children? Joseph must have had money to have an ass to be able to travel so steadily on to Egypt, instead of waiting to work his way.

To move around as he and Mary did – to the Passover at Jerusalem – also to have lost Jesus and returned for Him, makes you feel they were travelling in the style the wealthy Jews and Arabs still do, with a large retinue of servants and camels, etc. They naturally thought Jesus was with one or the other until they stopped and missed Him at meal time. To know the ways of the East is to understand more clearly. Jesus was lost for three days, and when they found Him it was with people of their own class as, naturally, Jesus as a boy would seek people of his own understanding instinctively, and so He went to the educated, not to the poor in tents and slums. Besides, being the child of educated and religious parents as we know Mary and Joseph were, he most likely knew of the religious and learned sect of doctors, and for them to have accepted Him shows He must have been fairly decently clad and spoken, or known beforehand. His desire for knowledge and the awaking of His spirit starts, as we are told, when He was twelve. It was curious that Jesus was lost and picked up at this age by a sect of high-thinking men; really, I think, showing that God never leaves go, for it is a scientific fact that it is best to catch a lad for his spiritual development and confirmation between the ages of twelve and thirteen. Jesus sought to learn and be well educated. The will awakens. Throughout all His preachings and teachings we see Him as a man of education and knowledge. We do not hear a word of envy in any of His teachings: "Render unto Caesar what is Caesar's," and also the parable of the good steward. Again we have, "Servants, obey your masters according to your service, not with eye service but with singleness of heart," and "Put them in mind to be subject to principalities and powers, and to obey magistrates, to be ready in every good work." "But avoid foolish questions and genealogies and contentions and strivings about the law, for they are unprofitable and vain." (St. Paul's words, not Jesus's).

Give up yourselves, but do not force others except by thought and power of thought – example. He never forced anyone; in fact He could not perform His miracles except "ye believed". It had to be a self-effort. When He said to the rich man, "It is easier for a camel to go through the eye of a needle," surely He meant because of the effort a rich man has to make for his soul. His wealth was his temptation for ease over his body, and so brings down his power of will. If his wealth is taken from him by force it is not bettering his, the rich man's soul, because it is not his effort. We all have different efforts to make for our souls to become likened unto God's, and so able to hear His voice, and communicate direct. A soul can only advance, as we see by Jesus' teaching, for the first effort to be that of the individual. Money is not everything, as Jesus proved by doing without it when He could have had it.

Yet He liked having, and admired nice things. His seamless coat, and the ointment Mary, his 'love', poured upon Him. A soul can only advance by will, and self-development. We cannot compare or envy: only unbiased helping and forgetting of oneself in the need of another, and by doing all that is within our power for the contentment of our spirit and the spirit and thought of others. Help, rather, to raise the thought of goodwill. Jesus gives us a very good example of the power of bad will when He lost His temper with the poor fig tree, which, after all, was not its fault. It was not its season to bear figs, but because it did not answer to the will – the vibration of thought – it was punished. We can move mountains if only we have exercised that power of will, which will so affect the atmospherics of the spiritual power and register on the thing we wish to effect. To register one must have power to feel: hence, Jesus loved Mary, and when Martha grumbled about Mary's lazy ways in not helping her prepare the meal for all the many guests, what did Jesus answer? "Martha, thou art careful and troubled in many things, but one thing is needful, and Mary hath chosen that good part, which shall not be taken from her."

As Jesus certainly liked luxury and nice things so, I feel, we ought to continue with and enjoy God's gifts, not being a slave to them, but by experimenting in science and using it to see more clearly God's power and how He works. Why, He gives us a hint – a carpenter: the beginning of using our brains and hands to invent things, which has gradually led up to all these inventions we have now.

As man has an instinct of God so he has to continue improving his methods of life. It is only by civilisation used with thought and the knowledge of a God working that we can get this world into one great brotherhood. Each helping the other, but by not taking away anything, rather by making each individual desire to give their best to the glory, and by seeking to find the way to communication with God. Look how Jesus prepared: starting from the age of twelve until twenty-eight He was learning and developing. Not until thirty, and after careful preparation and testing – the forty days' temptation – does He take up His work of showing the world that He is the Son of God, and how they may follow likewise. He tuned His will and power of thought until it could communicate with God, and it is that that matters.

If Jesus had to prepare for His work surely we have too, and because of His very human-ness therein lies our hope of forgiveness of sins, and our power and courage to continue to find this ethereal wave – the Holy Ghost, shown to us by Jesus the Carpenter in surely the same trade that has found out the miracle of wireless and started us on the great hope of one great brotherhood – one language, and one knowledge and communication with God. As it was in the beginning, is now and ever shall be – Thy will be done – as in heaven so on earth.

Conclusion

I have shown you a worldly Jesus, a loveable man such as our men, with a temper, not an indifferent man, and with a worldly love; with likes like our own, and yet with a power, which did things because He could commune with God. Do you notice, by the way, how He always sought solitude, quiet and height when He wished to concentrate most on God – catch His connection, His wave? Of course, it's our hope – our Father's too – that we, His children – after much learning and training may be likewise too. No reason for not being so if we learn, through faith and hope, because to the worldly Jesus, which will lead to love for our fellow men, to communicate and talk to God as we would to a father of great understanding and kindliness who, ultimately, through many worlds of perfecting ourselves, will make us as "His own likeness".

Having prepared the speech, she still felt nervous about giving it, till this incident occurred:

I used to keep on our veranda a large aviary of love-birds – parakeets … and during the fortnight while I was writing I lost one of my deep blue ones. I was very disturbed and prayed God to send it back. No parakeet came … I felt much worried at having to read out my belief and faith in God, so I prayed that what I had written should be correct and nearer what Christ meant us to aim for. I prayed for a sign from God that my writings had been guided by Him and …that the sign should be a blue bird – a blue love-bird. Needless to say, I expected to see my own quarrelsome parakeet and in fact did see a captured one in a Chinese garden nearby *[whose return they failed to negotiate]*. But God had a much more wonderful sign for me.

At the eleventh hour ... I climbed the hill to the Cathedral Hall, still looking and looking for a blue bird. As I reached the Cathedral, the doors of which were wide open so that you could look straight up to the Altar ... I looked and prayed again for strength and comfort, and as I turned my head away from the Altar, opposite me in the ... shrubs, no further away from me than six feet and eye level, were two magnificent blue rare Chinese birds, as big as crows, making violent love; the male was an especially fine blue, deep cobalt blue which a ray of sunshine brought out even more brightly. They had red beaks and two long tail feathers with an eye marking on the end of each. I stood and watched spellbound and then it struck me I must pray for a witness in this untrusting world of ours, so that I might explain if need be my faith in God. No sooner had I prayed than who should come out of the Dean's office than Mrs Black, one of the ladies Mrs Foster had introduced me to, and who had sat next to me. So I called her, and as she came the birds hopped down, but one hopped up again on a branch so that she might see, and at the same time there was a frightful clacking of a noisy magpie up on our right in the tall palms ... Looking up we also saw on our left, away up in a palm tree with a ray of sunlight shining on him, a peaceful white ringed dove – God's sign of the Holy Ghost. I had that sudden knowledge that is given to us. Here was the world – the magpie in the dark shade making a fearful noise and squabbling – God's signs opposite me – the blue birds – if only we have faith – and above, peaceably watching us, in the ray of light, His sign from the Heavenly world so often quoted in the Bible – for example at Christ's baptism.

Needless to say, I went into that Cathedral Hall with no fear – only a great comfort and thankfulness, and read what I had written by the aid of much prayer. It was well received, only one lady got up to go ... At the end of the meeting I was asked to read it again at another meeting so that it could be more discussed. Several ladies asked me for copies, which I was rather shy of supplying ...

Revelation

One Sunday morning my husband brought upstairs to our bed-sitting-room an Indian fortune teller. He had been lazing out of doors by the front door with nothing to do when the man offered to read his fortune for one dollar and my husband for the sake of a bargain said "and my missus too". So up they came to my surprise and it was decided to have mine done first. I gave him the day, hour and year of my birth, and also my names and my left hand. After counting the number of letters in my name and making other calculations with pencil and paper, he asked to see my left hand and said immediately, "Madam, you have had two children, one a miscarriage." I laughed and said, "No, only one." "Well, madam, you have a child now." I laughed again and said "No." "No laugh," he said, "very true, you have a child, you only carry two months and then you very sick, nearly die. By and by you have another, a world famous child, but you die, no matter." Of course we took it all as a joke. He then told my husband that he would not get his promotion, but would do much better when he left the Service than he had done in it, and that he was going to do something also for the good of his soul hereafter. A few days later he ran after my husband and said, "Master, I much troubled, your missus laughs for what I say very true – you look see your missus – she very, very sick soon." My husband came home and asked me when I had had my period last, as the Indian was so serious. We thought carefully, and then realised the Indian was right. I was with child and had carried already six weeks and had conceived unknowingly. My husband and I had been married for fourteen years, I had never had even the thought of a child excepting for our only son, John, who came to us within ten months of our married life. We had never even tried to prevent birth and so we had both long ago given up even thinking such a thing was possible.

Two months to the day I started a miscarriage in the middle of the night. The child never came away, instead I went septic and ran a temperature and was taken to Kowloon Hospital the next evening, Dr. Smalley said gaily, "Take little as you'll be back in a week." The next day I had my operation and Dr. Smalley said again, "Oh, everything near the entrance, you'll be home on Friday or Saturday," it then being Monday. But that week grew to over two months; I visited the operation table five times; my temperature went up again at the end of the first week, the night before I was due home, and so they carted me to the operating table to have a look, but I was so sore and painful that they had to put me under anaesthetic. Once again just as I was due out, up went my temperature. They removed the chart this time and insisted on me going to the theatre. But what they did I know not, all I know was that I very, very nearly died and that after this, my third visit to the theatre, I had a most wonderful revelation, which on coming round I remember, every word and detail, most vividly, even more than I have been able to write down for it was so vast, so full of feeling that words can hardly describe it. If I had been in England in a hospital I could never have written it but having a kindly Chinese Amah *[nurse]* sitting by my bedside I was able to ask for writing materials and a pencil and wrote all I had seen while my mind was still fresh. The following is a copy of what I wrote and saw and felt and knew had happened to me: -

I seemed to be standing on a brink or an edge of a vast outer world and yet one did not see the world one was standing on; the whole of your being was focused on a Great White Steady All-curing and embracing Light. You could not touch the Light and yet you felt a wondrous Love from it. It was opposite you and seemed to stretch as far as the eye could see whichever way you turned your head. It radiated feeling, sympathy and everything one desired – the Greatest Comforter. Everything seemed so very worthwhile. All one's suffering seemed so small and yet worth it. I remember saying to myself: "Why, this is 'the Love beyond understanding'!" One longed to jump off the brink into the Light; that is why I felt I was on a brink for I had a desire to jump off; in fact the desire to leap into it was immense but I was not allowed to, instead It spoke to me and also revealed to me the following:-

That YOU (everyone) are a being in which a spirit lives, bound to the earth, which has to rise through your feelings to God. A Being has feelings to do kind and unkind deeds but no real power to alter your Fate, which after all does not matter, provided you live to your highest ideals. But it is this power to 'feel' which matters. The Spirit of your Being is affected by this your power to give kindness and unkindness and also that of your Spirit's children later on. Your attitude towards mankind therefore counts.

I was shown the purpose of God which seemed to be after many trials, chances and lives, to try and mould us by our desire, into His Light. Here too I was shown the purpose of Life, the reason for suffering, and here was told I had a purpose to perform before I could pass on and that was to return to earth for 'childbirth', and that by my knowledge of death and lack of fear, and because of my love for my husband whom I must be prepared to love even though I thought it certain to cause death, so proving that the desire to return to God's Love is even greater than man's, for I fear it not but wish to reach it through my husband and he, I hope, through me.

I was then taken to a second Place, which I have called the Second Knowledge, for I seemed to go on up to it. It was the whole time a 'rising feeling'. Here there seemed to be two Heavens, or rather a first preparing Place, or lesser Heaven, embedded behind the Light. I could not see this Heavenly place but I could feel it, and hear the voices of the Spirits who had gone before. My mother's voice was one, astonishingly plain and easy to hear. She spoke not to me but to the 'Light' who spoke to me, and yet I knew she knew I was there although we could not see or communicate direct with each other. I was given to feel that this would have been wrong. We had to use the Voice of the Great Spirit of the Light, which was a pleasing voice, so soothing and pleasant that one only remembers it as such. I heard my mother begging the Light to explain that the first Preparing or Resting place was where we had to wait to be "forgiven our sins" by those to whom we had sinned. She begged for the end of all family quarrels and unkindnesses. She seemed to have to wait there before she could go to the Final Heaven, which seemed to be to unite in the Light itself – one with God – unto His likeness – and help in the great work of Comforting Love, and Bettering the World of Spirits so that they could finally join the Light too. This waiting seemed to distress her, as naturally her knowledge now made her more desirous to go on.

And then I was shown a wondrous thing. I saw people who had been allowed to 'dive into the Light' and as they passed through they seemed to give off many 'lesser lights' or Spirits: this was the rebirth of their Spirit children from their kind or unkind deeds on earth. It was as if they were rocks who had been blasted and some pieces broke into big bits, the kindnesses, and others into fragments, the unkindnesses, and each of these atoms was a 'light' but varying in size, the larger ones naturally having more chances when they return to earth to help on the work and help on their Parent Spirit, for these people did not lose their individuality – they went on – it was only that they left behind the results of their actions on earth by the rebirth of their Spirit children.

As the world gets kinder, so fewer births will take place, as the blasting of the better human beings will give off fewer fragments as they will have larger spiritual children. It seemed as if the person broke up and yet one knew the person had not, only his deeds, for it was explained that your kindly actions give larger spiritual force to the new mortals – unkindness lesser spiritual force. These children of your deeds on earth have to get through again to God – the Light. Meantime you wait hoping to win through to everlasting godliness by the Spirit atoms of your deeds succeeding on earth or wherever they are sent. So that should a baby be lost to an earthly mother, it is greatly welcomed by its Spiritual Parent who may be freed because of its quick return. Even a still born may have done some good to its mortal parent and yet returned early for the good of its Spiritual Parent. You also have to wait for the forgiveness of sins before you can continue the journey to the Grand Desiring Final. The forgiveness of sins is not from God but from men and women to whom you have sinned either by your ignorance or on purpose. No Spirit can jump off the brink into the Light unless he had fulfilled his purpose on earth – that is, the purpose for which God sent him out – nor can he hope for forgiveness of his sins unless he has forgiven, so freeing those who are still waiting in the 'After Life' imploring forgiveness and awaiting it in an agony of suspense – showing how united we are and how much depends on us.

The conclusion I reached was that we were to lead through Love and kindly deeds on this earth; it does not matter if your deeds of kindness are not returned here on earth, as they will swing you on twofold to the Heaven of Final Desire, for they will not only start off better men and women being born on earth through your spirit atoms being broken up into bigger spiritual force which in their turn will be able to succeed better on earth, and so by their success push you on and free you from the waiting place to the Final All-filling Perfection; which in itself is not a standstill but a great helping and recleansing power and Love to help those who are still struggling to better their spiritual selves. And again by your success you have freed someone who had passed on before you. In fact there is no end to the Spirit. It goes on and on – each time increasing in greatness. Its sufferings or Hell is to wait for its atoms to return to God to enlarge it and themselves.

We have power for those we love to help them on, as it is by Love and because of Love (this does not mean physical passion but spiritual) that we reach the height. For God is Love – the greatest and purest Love. By loving on earth, and by the purity and unselfishness of our love we can draw all men to God – open their eyes to the LOVE. For when they have passed through the knowledge, and stand on the brink and feel the purity of the Light on them, they will know the steadfastness, the greatness and depth of this Love for them, and realise how small in comparison is their own; they will leap gladly, willingly into this great cleansing Spirit of purifying Light and Love, fearing nothing, and then your purpose on earth will have been fulfilled and you may have the pleasure of joy in after life, instead of that long waiting period of suspense.

To give Love, or rather affect others by your Love, you can affect them by admiration for your purity of purpose and steadfastness, forgetting yourself in them and faithfully sticking to your highest ideals. By that it does not mean thinking all men wrong because they do not agree with you, but rather giving them your kindness for it is only by so doing you can win through with them and for your spiritual atoms' sakes.

<u>Earthly children</u> – and the meaning of 'all men are brethren' as we know not whose spirit atom we have in our children. One cannot, after they are born, affect the Spirit Atom of your child. For it has already been sent straight from God and is reborn in us according to our desire of kindness and unkindness before we women have 'quickened'. In other words they have already been born in the Spirit as soon as they 'quicken' in us. Our only power to affect them for better is during this waiting period before you 'quicken' and that by prayer and desire you may be given a large Spirit atom. You may help them on the road after they are born in the flesh in the same manner as one helps a stranger, but that is all that is in our power. Our Love for them will help them in their hour of need <u>if</u> it is big enough and has been pure enough to hold.

The chief thing to remember in dealing with children – and this I repeat again as it was so impressed on me – is that our children's spirits are not part of ours because they are of our flesh. No! Their spirits are the result of some other soul that has gone on and given rebirth to its Spiritual Atoms. We are merely the earthly receptacles in which those spirits are born again, but the size of the Spirit Atom, i.e. goodness of soul, may be according to our desiring and life before the child is due, and before it becomes a material human form – i.e. 'quickens'.

My original pencil writing has drawings instead of so many words and not so many explanations as I have given, as I was still so weak, only having just come round from my operation and yet feeling so strongly that I had to set down my vision in the quickest form I could so that I should not forget it – especially as there was so much to remember and so much detail, which I have tried to explain as ably as I can.

My mother evidently struggled while writing this to give an idea of time and place. She must have gone back to her original hospital sketches (which have since disappeared) and redrew these on the blank reverse side of her husband's DAILY ROUTINE ORDERS for the South Farnborough RAF station. Her diagram is on the upper half of one dated 12.5.31. Below the diagram she drafted her description of the 2nd knowledge, and had to complete it on the back of the Routine Orders for 11.5.31. The diagram is reproduced here:

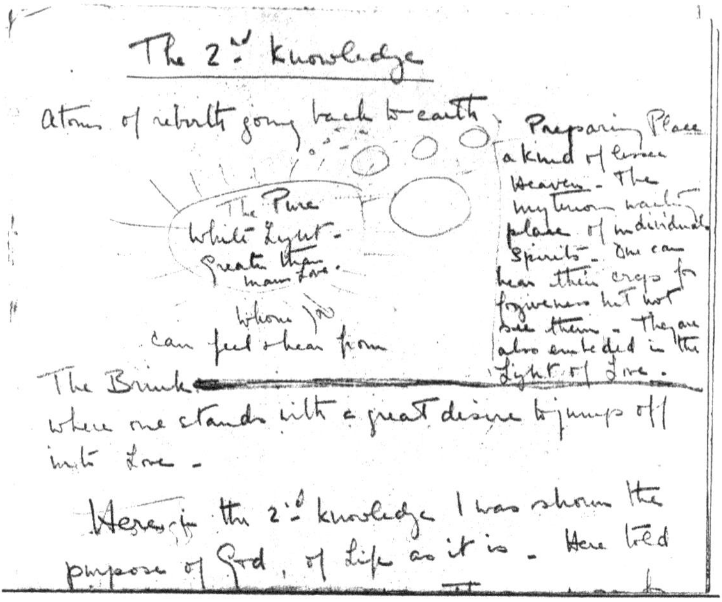

Although I was told my purpose for prolonged life I longed and longed to die; having seen the Light I hated the thought of earth again. God and His angels did a strange thing to make me come back – I kept half recovering from the anaesthetic and then sinking again. My heart felt hard and knotted and I tried not to recover. But the angels and spirits that had 'passed over' surrounded me. I could not see them but could hear their excitement to get me back. There seemed quite a number of them seeing me back to earth, for I had a descending feeling [*while being*]

followed by unseen hosts and they kept on saying to me: "Well, go back and see your baby. Just go back and see your baby first." It seemed as if only I would do that, then I might die. So I opened my eyes, feeling a dreadful weight on my heart; the amah's chair was empty; she had thought I was dying and had gone for the English doctor and nurse. As I looked up I saw on my bedpost near my pillow a blue ribbon to which a card was attached with a name I did not know: "Mrs Hodgkinson", hoping I would soon be better. "Ah!" I thought, "Now I can die. My year is passed, my baby born (blue ribbon) and this is someone I have made friends with meantime."

Then Dr. Smalley and the English nurse arrived, and I opened my eyes again in the hopes of seeing the babe which I thought they might bring to me. The doctor stood for some time looking out at Kai Tak (the Aerodrome) and I realised then that I had not had a babe, all was not over but about to begin, and yet I could not help smiling at the trick those unseen spirits had played on me. After the doctor had left me I asked the amah, who had also returned, to give me my writing block and a pencil, and I wrote down all I had seen while I was on the 'Brink', exactly as may be found with all my original notes and cuttings of verses of these days I have lived through, and which may be identified as such by the doctor and those who saw it both in Hong Kong and at home in England.

Just as I had finished writing Dr Smalley came in again. I gave him my writings and asked him to read them. I begged him not to destroy what I had written as I had been through and seen all that I had written down. He kept the papers for a few days and I begged and begged for their return. At last he returned them, saying: "There is no doubt you have seen something. It may be your religion, but not mine," or words to that effect. Anyway it distressed me greatly and I was very worried that I would not get back to the Light, so I prayed and prayed that night that God, the Light, would let me know if what I had seen was true and not make-believe, and that the Light was God – I asked for a clear message to be given in the text of the Morning Post paper – Hong Kong edition. How eagerly I waited for that Chinese paper-boy! Luckily he always called at breakfast time, came round to our bedsides. When I had opened the paper this is what I read: "Every good gift, and every perfect gift is from above and cometh down from the Father of Lights, with whom is no variableness, neither shadow of turning." James, Chapter I, verse 17 – *Hong Kong Morning Post*, 28th year, No. 7,217.

A few days after this my temperature again went up or it may be that it never came down as the doctor had ordered my chart to be kept out of my room. Anyway the doctor and my husband decided I had to go under again. I was weary of lying in bed – the days were frightfully hot and my pains only seemed to be getting worse. I felt inclined to shriek if a nurse touched my bed – the pain shot up, and if the doctor, who was kindness itself, came in again I felt I would scream. So I begged my husband to find the man who was this doctor's greatest rival and we decided on Dr. Black of Hong Kong, a private doctor who specialised in women's complaints. I was told I had to have an examination under an anaesthetic and both doctors would be present. As I was coming round from this anaesthetic a voice kept on saying to me so cheerfully: "You will tell Dr Black his son is quite all right and happy, won't you? You won't mind if they think you mad. You will tell him, won't you?" So persistently and yet this voice, that of a child, sounded such a happy voice. I promised.

When Dr. Smalley came to see how I was, I asked him if Dr. Black had had a son as he was "quite all right" and very happy and I told him of the persistent voice. He told me of the tragic circumstances of Dr. Black's only son's death and what great grief it caused his father.

Dr. Smalley then told me he thought I had had twins as otherwise he would have noticed the size of my left ovary, which he assured me had grown since he last had noticed it. It was very swollen. He was sorry but I would have to go under again but he hoped it would be the final operation. I was not a bit worried. I thought perhaps it was a twin and now I was going back to my Light, so I agreed, only saying I would like Dr. Black to do the operation, which Dr. Smalley agreed to, saying they would both be there.

He came himself to fetch me with the nurse and as I was being wheeled along I asked him to cut me open and have a jolly good look. No half measures; in fact, do what you like but let it be final. I came round from this operation perfectly naturally, nothing happened. I saw no one, felt nothing. I was told it was a major operation to which my husband had agreed. I asked the doctor to write down what he had done as I was certain before a year or so was up I was to have a baby and I would like to give the new doctor correct details. He did not tell me then what he had done, except saying that my husband had agreed. I did not care what he said or what had been done – all I knew was that I was more certain than ever that this babe had to be born. On my last day, as I went downstairs I refused to leave the hospital until Dr. Smalley had given me a typed and signed paper of what they had done and found; he gave me this:-

Mrs. Steele-Perkins

Had a miscarriage – 2 months pregnancy – which was offensive when patient was first seen on 2/4/30.

Uterus cleared out by me and extensive erosion cauterised. Left ovary was palpated under anaesthetic and found to be large; the right ovary could not be felt. Afterwards Mrs. Steele-Perkins complained of pain in left tube, and ran a temperature of 99-101 F.

I called Dr Black in consultation and he agreed patient should be opened. She was accordingly operated on by me, an ovarian 'cyst' – the size of a tangerine orange – was found and an 'acutely inflamed' tube. As there appeared to be little or no ovarian substance left I removed the tube and ovary.

The right tube and ovary were fibrosed and stuck down, there being practically no broad ligament on this side at all. Sir A.W. Lane had done one of his 'Kink' operations in this region when Mrs. Steele-Perkins was 16 years old. The appendix was removed at that time.

Mrs Steele-Perkins still has erosion which requires treatment.

Signed

Medical Officer in Charge

Kowloon Hospital

21/5/30

Shortly after returning to our rooms I had an attack of pain, and found my period was trying to start again with much difficulty. I sent for Dr. Black who told me that my periods would gradually end as a result of my operation and that I should never be able to have any more children. This worried me greatly, as how was I to fulfil my purpose according to my vision if I did not have a child? However, I prayed earnestly to God the Father of Lights, and after arising from my prayers had the sudden thought to look for and read the text of that day's morning paper. This was the answer I found to my prayer: "Only be strong and of a good courage." Joshua 1, verse 18. *Hong Kong Morning Post*, No. 7,250.

Now I felt very sure I was to have this baby and so cut out and have kept these answers to my prayers. I made up my mind not to worry any more over doctors and also gave up taking all medicines but do what nature and my instincts told me to do. This was to sea bathe and sun bathe, rest and eat simply, always having as much fruit as I could at all meals. I decided to return to England without my husband, who had to continue his service with his ship and go north to Wei-Hai-Wei.

Recovery

[The way she financed her trip home is omitted in the 1931 version and is taken from a 1950 version. The subsequent holiday in Parama with John is described in 1931 out of place, in the section she wrote after my birth, when explaining she wanted it published partly to help other new mothers. I have transposed it to its chronological place, as she did in a 1950s' version.]

As one may imagine, the expenses of my illness and return passage might have embarrassed us greatly, but again a far-seeing and good God helped. Mother had left £300 in ready cash to each of her seven surviving children. This money was sent out to me just at this time and with it I was able to pay all our outstanding debts and expenses and buy several beautiful things in memory of my mother and China, as well as select the route home which I had always longed to travel: that via Peking, Japan, Vancouver, the Rockies, Banff, Niagara Falls, Montreal and Quebec. After my husband left I was invited to stay with Dr. Black and his wife, who had lost their son. I stayed with Dr and Mrs Black and then with the wife of the Colonel of the Royal Garrison Artillery. This lady decided to come home with me and so share a state cabin on the

Canadian Railway and halve our expenses as much as possible. We had a most enjoyable trip, arriving in England a week before John, my son, had to say goodbye to his Preparatory School. *[My mother never forgot this trip so my grandmother's money was well spent!]*

How glad John and I were to meet again – although worried with difficulties in regard to finance and a home. The £300 had nearly gone, but I still had £20 for the holidays. My husband's father was too ill to have us. I soon realised London hotels would swallow up that £20. We decided to go to France as the exchange was in our favour. We found a small pension at Parama where we could board and feed three meals a day, bath, inclusive for £10 a month, provided we shared a room. John was nearing fifteen years. "Let's, Mum. We'll manage."

I found sharing a room perfectly easy as he proved to be a most thoughtful and modest youth, keeping always to his side of our improvised screen, generally getting up first, etc. What a happy holiday, ever to be remembered. We would lie and chat with the windows wide open, stars twinkling from the deep blue sky, the smell and sound of the sea gently lapping the shore. All past sorrows and home sickness came tumbling out of this reserved boy's mouth; he who never once had written to complain. "You were so far away. I knew by the time my letter reached you my worries would be over, so why worry you with them."

We spoke of all the subjects that most puzzled a lad as he blossoms into young manhood. I realised the great opportunity that kind Fate had given me just before my only son was to go to his Public School and decided to tell him of God's precious gift of creation. Lying there in the quiet of the night each sheltered and separated by darkness, it was easy to speak to him and say: "Darling, soon your voice will be cracking and you will feel all kinds of new sensations which mean that God thinks you are now man enough to take on greater responsibility, that of His greatest gift to us here on this earth, the power of creation. As a baby you were baptised and other people were responsible for your sins and upbringing. Now you are to be confirmed, as we think you are old enough to know good and evil. God, when He gives you this gift, also expects you to be old enough to guard it from all harm and dirtiness, and keep it for your perfect love, blessed by a marriage service."

I then explained to him all about bad women and trials he must pass through to prove his worth. I frightened him by telling him of the fearful illness he could get and told him to keep himself well exercised with playing games, walking, etc., and, above all, cleanliness ... We women bear the fruit, you men the pollen. Only as animals and man have greater power of sense than flowers we need no bee or insect to help us. Instead the help is given by a wonderful love; and you will be the most ashamed man on earth if, when you find your perfect woman, you have spoilt your most precious gift. I told him nice people did not talk of these things publicly as they were holy and precious and kept like we keep our religion and thoughts of God, sacred, but if ever he was worried or wished to ask anything he could talk to his parents, or his headmaster or a doctor, but not to other boys and women in a trivial fashion. He thanked me most charmingly and we became even greater pals.

During the day we associated with the other guests of the hotel, all French of the bourgeois type. There were a number of boys and girls of John's age. He soon became very popular, playing tennis or cricket on the sands, thoroughly enjoying everything and trying so hard to learn French.

What an excellent summer! We were able to bathe twice a day, resting and sun-bathing. We did a good deal of walking, exploring different villages and towns. I realised if I had to fulfil my purpose for returning to earth – that of childbirth again, I must try and get strong so as to do it well. When I bathed I used to tread the sea-water a great deal, doing the goose-step, only sufficiently deep in the water not to be observed, and as the beach was a long safe stretch of sand I would go a long distance, allowing the waves to gently massage my stomach muscles so as to strengthen them and succeeded to such perfection that I soon became abnormally well and strong.

The holidays came to an end only too soon and money too grew terribly short. After paying the bill and the outside porter for the luggage we found we really had nothing left, not even a tip. John undertook to get the luggage aboard. Soon I was surprised by a porter bringing the cases to my cabin, and still more surprised to hear a man next door say to my son, "Thank you most awfully. It's very good of you I am sure." "Not at all, Sir," replied John. "I will help you get your little load off in the morning again if you wish." The strange man thanked him and tipped the porter.

"Well, Mother dear," said triumphant John, "and that was done for nothing." "How on earth did you manage?" "Luck. I saw a fellow surrounded with luggage, a helpless wife, nurse and two babies. He could not speak French. Nor can I, but still, better than he could. He was getting really bothered and so I went up to him and said to him 'May I help you, Sir? I've got to get my Mother's luggage seen to, so I will do yours for you if you will point out your things.' And this he did, and luck was again with me; he and his wife are in the next cabin. The porter thinks we are all one happy family."

Across from the boat to the train, without a penny but many smiles and many thanks – that was John. He grinned himself out of difficulties. We returned to England two days before he was due back to school, which was on September 23rd 1930. My husband returned from China on September 25th.

Realization

What was extremely astonishing was that my periods, which had practically finished excepting for a day or so, as Dr. Black said they would, now commenced again. I had one quite good period and felt much better for it, and no further pain. I had another short period in October, about three days ... nothing more. In November being stationed at a new Camp *[Farnborough]* we were asked to a Mess Dance in our honour. We went. After dancing once or twice I felt fearful pains coming on. Luckily I was with my husband and immediately insisted on going home and to bed. I was not going to allow my period to start again. I felt certain, although I was only five days late I was with a seed. Luckily, the people who had dined us were old friends, and so my husband asked them for the name of a good woman's doctor. They told us that quite close to us, two or three minutes away, lived a Harley Street specialist for cases like mine *[Doctor Moss]*. Had not God provided for me wonderfully! I was able to go to this man after I had rested a further three days as I was not going to allow him or anyone to prod me in case they should upset the seed. I believe I waited in bed a week before I went to see this doctor and as soon as I saw him I told him of the Light, its message, and that I was certain I had a child. He said it was too early to say but if I wished to know at once so as to take every care, there was a test I could have and the result would be told me in nine or ten days' time from a place in Edinburgh. I agreed. This man also believed in my Light but not in my death. His father was a great friend of Professor Huxley's, so I felt happy at once. Death did not worry me but I knew it was useless to argue. He asked me if I had told my husband my fears. Of course I had not as he naturally would not wish to cause my death. I had told him I expected a child and nothing would persuade me to rid myself of it. My husband felt that this was impossible as before leaving China he had seen Dr. Smalley and been told it was impossible for me to have one.

Dr. Moss wrote to me and asked to see me. He told me the reply from Edinburgh was "Yes" and that he wished to see me through. He wrote my husband a very charming letter. [*The letter was not in the original account but as my mother saved it, I include it. It shows how doctors then had to adjust their bills and could be uncertain of their income.*]

> Dear Mrs Steele-Perkins,
>
> I hope that you are feeling better and staying in bed. I will be in to see you on Friday morning.
>
> In reply to your letter of 15th, I do not want your husband to worry about expenses because I mean to look after you for what he can afford and when he can afford it. My fees up here are from 50 to 100 gns [Guineas, 21 shillings] for confinements but near my home in Farnborough I suggest 30 gns and I will charge one guinea for ante natal exams and modify this if he finds it too much. You will have to have expert attention in any case and you may not after all be pregnant, I cannot swear to it yet in spite of the very strong evidence. In any case tell him not to worry and to discuss it with me when he likes.
>
> Yours sincerely,
>
> Lawton Moss

So my prayer had been answered, and answered with such care and love. Everything I wished for I had, it just came to me. The house we were sent to live in was a very up-to-date married quarters in Farnborough with everything in it for a baby. Electric light and power, plenty of hot water and airing cupboards, etc. Nice large rooms full of sun, an easy, broad staircase with a double rail. I never had to advertise for servants – a good cook-housekeeper and her very kind and hard-working husband came to our hotel and asked if we wished for two servants to run our married quarters for us. I asked her name, she replied

"Perkins", the same as ours. I took them at once without a reference; of course God had sent them to me. I trusted them completely and set myself to get the house so well run by them that I need do nothing at all except the flowers; and even in this Perkins used to carry and empty the large vases and bowls for me. I took such great care of myself, denied myself no end of pleasures, I never went out except for walks as I found the car too unnerving and so would not go out in it until the seventh month had been safely reached. I rested a great deal. Breakfast in bed until 10:30 a.m., took small walks and towards the end just walked in the garden for ten minutes at a time. My husband, as luck would have it, had brought home two long Chinese chairs; I had one in the sitting-room/study and the other for the garden. I went from chair to chair, sewing, reading and writing this my book. He also had brought home some silk which I used for baby clothes, etc. I encouraged my husband to go out to golf a great deal and to be great friends with John. I did not mind being alone as I felt when I had gone they would not miss me, so I spent many days alone. We were at a new station and as I did not go out I naturally met very few people.

The manuscript book ends soon after this point. After adding "Now I wait – ready for God's will," *she gives a list of her witnesses, names and addresses. She adds*: I have written this for the comfort of my husband and children that they may believe and not grieve for me for there need be no sorrow or mourning but a great joy and thankfulness that things are as they are and a great comfort to all men ... *She continues with her desire to have her book published and her instructions concerning any royalties. She finishes:* ... my life on earth has indeed been a happy one, blessed by a loving husband and the most comforting and helpful of sons, John. We are sure all to meet again with an even better understanding. *She signs if off on June 27th, 1931.*

The manuscript resumes on September 16th 1931 with an account of my birth, but the typed book first has an account of subsidiary visions during her pregnancy.

I must mention some curious things that happened to me while I was so looking forward to death and the birth of my child. It was during the early stages before I had quickened that I seemed to sleep very little and on waking felt I had been away somewhere. I used to see 'Soul Lights' like the pieces of good and bad kindnesses of people's deeds while on earth, meaning 'the rebirth of souls' as seen in my vision. Some of these 'lights' were very big and I longed to have a child with a great big soul light. I used to pray a good deal that my babe should have this big soul. I spoke to my husband about these 'lights', although I knew he would and did laugh at me, but I had to mention these things then so as to get witnesses that things were as I am describing them, the whole time hoping that my experiences might be a help to others not so blessed.

Still it certainly was curious that after I quickened I never saw another "light" and slept much more soundly. Thinking and reading things over, of course I now realise it was because the soul was in me and no longer wandering, yet the night my babe was due I woke with a great feeling of blessedness and comfort, and saw a great light which I felt was my wee one's soul that I had been permitted to see. I know the comfort of it was so great that I turned over and hugging myself with joy slept soundly. Another curious thing was the morning just before I first felt a wee slight movement, I saw many small lights flying towards me like birds with outstretched wings and I felt they were bringing me something. I believe I told the doctor, but I did not feel a movement until a fortnight later when again I saw these bird lights flying towards me. I tried to put a meaning on it then and thought that a fortnight meant two months, as I told the doctor. Anyway, I knew it had something to do with the birth of baby and did not realise the connection until the time of her birth, which I will describe later.

I had yet another dream, very vivid, so much so, that I wrote to Dr. Moss, not waiting to tell him. I woke one night ... with a clear knowledge of having heard my mother's voice and having seen a child of six years or so sitting on my mantelpiece. It seemed to be a boy *[later altered to child]* with plenty of spirit and life, tall, slight build, the very active type. My mother asked me if I would have her soul atom child, and gave me to feel it was to be born two years after the child I now carried. I then saw myself seriously ill and was asked even should this happen to me would I still be willing to have this baby: to which I agreed. *In one manuscript, but not the final typed version, she adds:* I then saw myself dying, Now none of this happened.

In the typed book she goes on to describe the miscarriage she had two months after my birth, to which she thought this must refer. In her 1950s' accounts she gives some more details: the room had pale green walls and two windows. She saw first two men. One was her husband, looking as tired and weary as she herself felt. The other, of slighter build, had his back to her, so she could not recognise him. Was he the doctor? She then looked down the room and saw the child on the mantelpiece. The details are corroborated by Dr Moss's reply which she gives in the 1950s and which I repeat here. The short and confused account of what was a "vivid" dream makes me feel that Dr Moss asked for his reaction to her letter to be omitted when he read the book as one of her 'witnesses'.

Dr. Moss, when he got my letter describing the scene I had interpreted as "my death bed", came round full of wrath. No mother, he assured me, would wish her daughter's death. "For pity's sake, give a little thought to your husband's feelings too. Will he not feel a murderer if you die in childbirth? I warn you if you are going to make up your mind to die, I will hand you over to someone else. I won't be the other man." He saw my nurse *[it was common then to hire a nurse to stay for a month from a week or so before the expected birth]* and gave private orders to her that the birth was to take place in John's blue room. He did everything he could to make me of a better mind, although I was cheerful – not fearing death – having known it.

Only a girl!

Her manuscript draft shows she started this section when I was two months old, and she proceeds directly to giving the details of my birth. Fortunately this was much easier than John's birth, because she knew what to do and what to expect. When she revised it for typing, she decided the section had two purposes: "to show how God remained to help and comfort me, and also to help other new mothers to bear their pains." She continues by recollecting how much she suffered in the birth of John, through her ignorance, and her ignorance also at marriage. This led her to explain how she had described the facts of life to her son, which I have moved to its chronological place. She also tried to ensure the new child was not left in ignorance.

When I knew the baby was arriving – John just fifteen – I naturally told him that Dad's and my love was to meet with a reward soon, that of another child. He could not have been kinder and nicer to me. He never let me stoop but ran and fetched and waited on me most sweetly. For example, it was a very hot summer and his father told him to throw up the sitting room window to which I had my back. He carefully opened it at the top only. His father said: "Oh, throw it open at the bottom, John, as well. "Dad, I am thinking Mother might feel the draught on her back."

April was cold but the government, during the depression, told all camps to economise. My father did so by cutting the coal allowance, to his house as well. John saw to it that a full scuttle was kept in my mother's room in case of need. Some friends arrived on a Sunday afternoon and my father told John to light a fire. He tried to do so rather unsuccessfully with wood and coke. My father was reminded of the full scuttle of coal when going to bed, and cuffed him for being a blind fool. The boy replied: "Yes, I knew the coal was there ... It's mother's; she may need it."

I impressed on the lad if anything happened to me and his father, he must promise to tell it all about God's gift of creation before the child went to school and had his ideas spoilt. "But Mother, what if it is a girl?" So then I explained about girls to him and how they knew. "If it is a girl you can tell her, instead of letting her be frightened." "Oh yes, of course I can," he replied, "you need not worry. I will see she knows in the way you have told me." So my mind was at rest over this most important question.

Sept. 16th, 1931

Baby Gladys Mary is now two months old. She was born on July 16th at 11.00 am (Greenwich Time). On Wednesday night I woke at about 11.30 p.m. feeling I had been somewhere, and reassured all was going to be just perfect. I felt a great blessing and a great happiness. I saw one large steady light, which I knew was the size of my child's soul and after murmuring a prayer of thanks and assurance turned over and hugged myself with refreshing joy and knowledge of well-being and slept soundly until 3.45 am. I woke to find my waters had burst. *Her husband woke and they called the maternity nurse, who had been with them since July 6th, just after 4 am. She confirmed things had started and alerted the doctor. My mother rested peacefully thinking of all the wonderful places she had been in. As the dawn arrived, she noticed spots of white flash by very swiftly up and down the garden.* I thought they were "lights" as I had seen when I quickened. I looked hard and found they were swallows; their upper feathers being black you could not see them so clearly in the half-light against the house opposite and trees, only their white breast and underwing which caught the early sun's rays as it was about to appear. How excited they seemed! Such hosts too – their first appearance to us. I could not but feel delighted at seeing them for they of all the birds were my husband's and mine, our "love-birds". During the war, when we were parted, if we saw a swallow we thought of each other ...

The doctor arrived *[after she had had a bath and breakfast in bed]* and soon left as I really was quite comfortable and wished only to be left alone in peace so that I could think with my eyes closed of all the happy days I and my husband had had together, and what a feast of lovely landscapes I had seen in this world of ours – Egypt – China – Japan – the Rockies – Niagara Falls and Canada. It was strange how the past pictured itself again for me and took my mind off myself. The doctor arrived again at 9.30 am with his large bag full of tools, etc. ... He fixed a chloroform apparatus to my bed which I could use if I needed it. Nurse brought her knitting in to sit beside me. ... The swallows were getting more and more excited; they kept flying up towards my window. One particular one tried hard to get in. It screamed at the window-pane – just as if it wanted to come in and see what everything was about. Two others started to build their nest under my eaves. Was it not curious, for it was the only place round the house that they built, against my wall, and starting on the morning baby was arriving; they didn't stay long, just four or five days. I don't think they even laid an egg, as much as to say: "Now you are better we are off. We mean 'Love'."

She was so placid that at 11.15 the doctor was going to phone another, in case a Caesarean was necessary. No sooner had he gone than the fiercest pains came and Nurse ... said she could see the head and rushed out of the room to call him back. ... I obeyed instructions, pressing and holding back. As twelve sounded on the bells my darling cried. ... The doctor told me a girl; he knew I had expected a boy. The blue ribbon on my bed after my vision made me think it was to be a boy. "However" he said gaily, "perhaps your next will be a boy." No." I replied, although I would quite welcome another, "perhaps baby will produce the child of my vision, for I may not be great enough in spirit."

[It was the Indian fortune teller who suggested her next child would be world famous – the vision only told her to return for childbirth. In 1931 my mother assumed world fame was impossible for a girl. Later, after I had been to Cambridge University, she changed her mind and when I was toying with the idea of applying for a job in the Foreign Office, thought I might become Foreign Secretary, apparently not realising that this required becoming an MP, a path I had no intention of following! Strangely, long after her death in 1981, research I led in Kenya and the resulting book (1994) of which I was the lead author, became internationally known in its field. It changed thinking and is still much quoted. In this limited sense I was internationally known. As the Indian had also said, 'You die, no matter.' She knows now, I trust, in the life above.]

... We called her "Mary" after both our mothers who have "passed on". She was christened very quietly in the soldiers' chapel. A friend sent a small bottle of water from the River Jordan as a complete surprise, which arrived two or three days before the christening. *[Some paragraphs follow on the way I learnt to walk and talk, etc. I was the perfect baby every mother has!]*

Three months after she was born I had the miscarriage already spoken of, which left me an even fitter woman. *[She reports her feeling of energy and joy at this time including]* more enjoying married life and knowing I now can give even more satisfaction, for since Mary's arrival our understanding, which was good before, is very much more perfected now. I have not been near a doctor since and hope I will never have to be again or my baby either. In fact, I am a new woman.

Needless to say I still look forward to joining "the Light", but it is not for us to take our lives but to live them to the best so that when THE time comes we may leap gladly knowing we have done of our best. No matter how poor that may be in this world's eyes He will understand, having seen our struggles and knowing our soul's start in life and our weaknesses.

PART III

SACRIFICE

John's accident

This is taken from a 1950s' account. A note says that it was written immediately after the last events she describes here, when she could not sleep, but her draft has disappeared.

Shortly after Mary's birth her father, who believed greatly in setting the good example, went flying. He was a C3 man, that is to say, passed as medically unfit to fly, but nevertheless he did so, as he said he disliked ordering other men to do it especially those nearing his own age, and not doing so himself. He tried to make it a practice to go up once or twice a month.

On this occasion he was not feeling too well but, as he always felt better in the air, he decided to go and practise landings. John asked to come with him but this he refused; although he used to take the lad up, he felt uncertain of himself that day and was determined to try and make himself more assured and self-confident. As he was about to take off an airman asked to come with him; to this he agreed as he did not like to refuse the man, or to damp his zeal. Off they went. It was bitterly cold. Looking down he saw machine after machine come out to go up. He sailed around for forty minutes, trying to land in a clear field. His hands were numb as he had not taken his gloves, thinking he was only going for ten minutes or so. He felt he must land. Just as he was about to land he saw another machine and cut out of its way too near the ground. His wing caught and he crashed. Something had hit the airman on the head. Getting no reply from him, he looked over and saw the man was seated under a leaking petrol tank. He got out and pulled the airman away. He had had the presence of mind to turn his engine off as soon as he realised what was to happen. Luckily the airman recovered and neither of them suffered more than a few cuts and bruises about the head.

John, who had been watching the aeroplanes on his bicycle, raced over to the scene of the accident.

"Was that the Wing Commander?" he asked an airman. "Yes, sir." "By George, I must have a bit of the wreck as a memento," and he took a piece of the broken propeller. He then cycled home, having heard that his father had gone back home. There he saw the Doctor and his father partaking of whisky and soda. "Hello, Dad. That was a fine crash. Here's a bit of the propeller."

This was too much for the old man and he retired to bed, to be kept quiet. I had been out at a Mothers' Union meeting and on going up to our room was relieved to see my man reading the paper. He was back at work the next day. Nevertheless, Headquarters were none too pleased and said being a C3 man he had no right to fly and would have to pay for the damaged plane. Luckily he managed to sell it to the Experimental people. Nevertheless, he was moved from Farnborough to the Air Ministry, out of temptation. Here he was told he could not get the promotion that would allow him to stay on because of the bad condition they considered his heart to be in. He therefore need only wait on *[till his 45th birthday in August 1933]* to get his full pension.

The move meant we had to move out of our quarters and find a house of our own. No one was sorrier than John. He had made great friends with the men in the Camp, especially the wireless section. He would be lost all day in the holidays, learning all he could from the Camp. He became very keen on everything electrical in wireless and flying. The Head of the Experimental branch lived next door. He had two sons of his own. John liked the family and grew keen over flying. He thought the Experimental branch with wireless attached would be the thing of the future, so he decided to work for that. Every spare penny he had he spent on trying to create something. The neighbour allowed him to use carpenter's shop, but this opportunity was lost with his father's compulsory move.

The search for a new home ended in a small modern house built on a big estate surrounded by fine grown trees. The garden was a field but as all three of us were keen gardeners we soon transformed it. John's disappointment at leaving Camp could be seen by his small room being made into a workshop. The walls were covered with diagrams and notes on all the subjects he loved, but which he had soon to give up, due to the strains of work for examinations which his father saw as necessary qualifications. I too had to give up my servants. My time was taken up with looking after the baby and the housework, cooking and laundry for the family, as my husband pleaded poverty owing to the move. I could have no days off except in the holidays when John, then aged 16, offered to act as nurse to little Mary while I had a day in town. He would even change the baby's nappies, give her bottle and sing her to sleep in his cracking base voice. He even started to give her nightly bath if we were a little late getting back from an outing together.

I was most anxious for John to be confirmed. This had been put off owing to the death of the Headmaster, a man John liked well, and who returned the compliment. John for some reason did not care for the new and younger man, but his father liked him. I wrote to the Master saying I wished the lad to be confirmed that term at Winchester Cathedral where, by coincidence, both I and my husband had been. We both had been at schools in or near Winchester. Unfortunately our wish never was fulfilled. Halfway through the term, on a Tuesday morning, we received a letter from the Headmaster that our son had suffered a 'slight accident', and would have to keep to his bed for a short while. I was all for going at once to see what it was, but his father said he had work to do and hated asking for leave. He would phone from the town and hear what it was all about. He phoned and decided that there was no hurry. We would go at the weekend. The boy had been playing some foolish game, about which he would not speak, and had been badly hurt but nothing serious.

When we arrived at the school the Headmaster had not remained in to see us and John was at the School Sanatorium with the School Matron, who did not say much, thinking we knew the extent of the damage. John, with both hands bound up, greeted us with his usual cheerful smile, saying his legs were burnt as well, but making very light of it all and never once complained. Poor John, his pluck was his undoing. We left still in ignorance of the extent of his burns or their seriousness.

The old school Doctor was away with 'flu and a young up-to-date man had been called in. He had given John the correct modern treatment of tannin spraying. The older man, on his return, was horrified at the blackness, never realising how much better the burns already were, and ordered hot fermentations to be put on to take off all the blackness.

Poor, poor John. Matron said she was surprised the Head did not hear his shrieks of pain, and yet they continued this cruel treatment until we visited again, which was only at the weekends.

John, feeling sensitive to his father's anger at bringing all this on himself and missing his work, never once complained of his treatment or the pain he suffered. He never even looked ill. He never had much colour at the best of times. His father, not believing a lad could be quite so resigned or reticent about a pain such as a burn, never realised the depth of the damage or bravery of his son until weeks afterwards.

How little the Headmaster and I realised the extent of his burns is shown by the Headmaster's letter dated 9th November 1932:

> John seems to be getting on quite as well as can be expected, though I am afraid it will be at least a fortnight before he is about again. I note what your doctor says about the necessity for stretching his legs and I will mention this to our doctor.
>
> We have about half a dozen boys or so who are being prepared for confirmation. The first class is held on November 17th, and I will see that John joins them if he is fit by then, but even if he misses the first, he can quite well join up the following week.

It never occurred to us to ask for an altered treatment. His father's and Headmaster's attitude were that the lad had brought it on himself and had no one else to thank for his sufferings. His father was more worried over the amount of work the lad was missing and begged for his studies to be continued and papers set, but this was not done very seriously by the masters. The lad spoke of his loneliness in the small cell-like room, and asked if he could have his gramophone, which was brought to him; but he could not use it because of his bound hands, and had to rely on the matron's goodness. How he must have felt people's careless cross words because he said to me when his hands were better: "Don't put things out of reach, Mother dear. She (the Matron) gets so fed up if I have to call her for anything." And again, "Do tidy up the room. She always swears if I drop anything, and I can't move to pick it up yet." No one ever thought of bringing him in flowers. He only had mine when I came to brighten up the empty flat walls. There was a bed, a table, the fire on the same side as the head of his bed, so that he could not even see its brightness. The deprivation must have been severe for a boy who loved colour and flowers especially. He had done some beautiful pastel drawings of flowers just before his accident. He lay in that room alone from October 29th until the end of the Christmas Term, December 22nd.

Just before the end of the term we were requested to fetch him away as the school was to be shut down. We thought he must be up and better to be able to be moved. His father went down alone in our small Austin 7. One of the front seats had been removed so as to allow the lad to stretch his legs. I stayed behind with the baby to make more room in the car. When his father arrived in the early afternoon he was greatly surprised to find the school already closed. The Headmaster had gone and only the old matron and John were waiting for him at the "San". They had great difficulty in getting the lad in without more help. John could still only wear his pyjama top and a dressing gown, his lower limbs being swathed with bandages. He begged his father to drive slowly, feeling every jar. When he got home, he was helped out by both parents, so pale but smiling. He greeted me, saying: "I am glad that ride is over. It was most unpleasant."

I had put his bed down in the dining room, knowing he could not face the narrow stairs. As I helped him I saw that his bandages were soused in blood and matter from the jolting of the car. He should have had an ambulance. We sent for the local Doctor at once. The Doctor arrived quite promptly and asked me to unwrap the legs, as he did not wish to touch so septic a wound, having other cases to attend. I scrubbed up as I always did, both before and after the dressing, and begged my husband to remain in the room. I thought it was high time he realised how much the lad had suffered and was still suffering instead of always being told "he had no one else to thank" and given work to do and cursed when he failed to do it.

The wound had been dressed by using one large piece of lint 3/4 yard by 9 inches wide, smeared with camphor ointment, very heavy and difficult to get off as in places it had stuck. Lifting it tore the very sensitive skin that was trying to heal. "What he needs, Doctor, is a bath of liquid paraffin or something like it," I remarked. "I used to be put in a bath of salt water," said John. "How? Just your legs?" "No. Get in as if I was having a proper bath." "With all the poison and pus floating around?" "Oh, they weren't as particular as you are, Mother dear. You're so gentle after what I have been through." At last the legs were exposed. His father had to go out of the room, feeling and looking completely ill at the sight. The Doctor and I were horrified. It was terribly septic and almost showed the bone at the back of the knee. In fact we could not make it out if it was bone or pus. It was very, very deep. "And they told us, Doctor, he had only a patch the size of the palm of a man's hand." "That's the patch," said John. "This other leg and the rest of the burns they call scarred, but it hurts like the Dickens, nevertheless." "Oh, John, why, why did you not tell us?" "I thought you always knew. I thought the Head had told you. Besides, the less I think of it the better I can bear it, and if you have it night and day one tries not to think of or discuss it. It only makes things so much worse."

Bravely spoken, yes, but what did it lead to? His foolish parents only learnt from seeing that wound and the silent cheerful bravery of the lad during the two days he was waiting to go to a hospital, how much he could suffer and control his show of pain. The Doctor ordered he go to the hospital at once and said he very much feared he would lose the leg. He left me to redress the wound, which I did in strips of very well-greased ointment.

John looked forward to hospital, anything to have correct treatment and care at last. While his father tried to get him into the 'London', I dressed the wounds twice the next day. Once in the morning when the baby generally slept, but she was awakened by impatient tradesmen who came when I was in the midst of my operations. Being scrubbed up I continued and the baby yelled and tradesmen rang while I and John were both on tenterhooks over this fearful dressing. How very, very brave he was. He tried to cheer me by talking and telling me how good I was, so gentle, etc. It took me nearly two hours to prepare the lint and boil up the scissors and knife, and then to clear away and make his bed and disinfect again. It had to be repeated in the evening.

When his father returned and said he had failed to get the lad in anywhere, I spoke most seriously: "Do you realise what you're asking? I am not super-human; I can't cook, clean a house and care for and feed a baby as well as shop and do for the lad. You must get him somewhere. If you can't a hospital, well then a home, or get me a nurse; but we have not the gadgets a hospital has and he has suffered too much, curse us for fools." "But I've tried." "Well you jolly well have got to do something.

What is the use of belonging to a family of Doctors if they can't help you now?"

"I will try Guys." Many of his family had graduated there and they had a bed. They advised the Accident Ward – "Ashley Cooper". A private ward would be too lonely for so young a fellow. They sent him to see the best specialist. John was to go the next day.

How relieved we were. All the family went up to hospital with him in the wee car – minus a seat. I sat behind the father who drove, with the baby on my knee; John next to me, his bad legs raised on the suit-case which took the place of the seat, well wrapped in blankets and eiderdown, cushions and hot water bottles. It was a raw cold day, sleeting; and waiting in the long draughty passage for the lift, after perhaps a too warm car drive, John caught a cold and had to wait for his operation.

He entered Guys on December 24th. The wards were gay with Christmas decorations and much to his joy he got his own Christmas presents which I had managed to smuggle into the car. I had given them to the Sister to give him next morning, and the kindly Sister had added some of her own for him. He was well enough to enjoy the fun of the day and of Boxing Day, when the Students entertained the patients. His better leg healed and the septic one they made cleaner, and so the cold did good as it gave him a chance to answer to a less painful treatment. How thankful he was; even merrier and fuller of smiles when he saw his parents. But nevertheless he had to have two grafting operations and even then change treatment as he would answer so far, and then stop, and again something else had to be tried to get his body to respond – he found it hard to pull up. His father was able to see him every luncheon hour, and much to his worry found the lad had not done the work he had set him to do or even read the task he had set. He would come back and complain to me how little the lad cared. "I found him asleep with the book in his hand, and when I cross-questioned him he knew nothing. He reads so little." Ad all the while the poison oozed and oozed, and the lad just could not; after the slightest effort he would fall into a doze. "Don't worry him," I pleaded, only to be told I was a very foolish woman.

The Sister refused to worry the lad or be his task master. "Oh, he's all right," she would say. "I see him with his books often, don't I, John?" John liked her. But in spite of all the doctoring they could not get the wound to close, and the Doctor and nurses were worried. It was late April. He was up, hobbling, but not trousered as yet. "Oh Mother, I do so long to get home. I am getting so tired now. I feel I will never get well." I saw the Matron and asked her if the lad could come home. I realised I would need help at home. A sister heard of a German girl aged 19 who wished to learn English and would help with the house and baby as one of the family. A companion for John, too, I thought. The father was against it all. "We have got him in Hospital. Don't take him away till he is healed." "The Doctor agreed with me; a change of air and environment might do the trick. Try and see; he could go to "out patients" once in ten days.

It was now 2nd May. The father went up to bring the lad home. I went up to town too to fetch the German girl who had just arrived from Germany, leaving Mary next door with friends she knew. God in His blessing sent this stranger, Lotty, to fit in well with the family. She was willing to learn and willing to amuse John and take her share with the baby, Mary. John's leg still had to be dressed and exposed to the sun for so many minutes each day. He used to lie in a sun trap veranda, sheltered by glass at the sides, on the same long chair I had used during Mary's coming. Lotty would try to help him with the lessons which his father would set and correct for him each evening.

Curiously, just at this time, I heard from both the Doctors who had operated on me in China. I had written to them telling them of the book I had written and was surprised to hear that they had both come to England for "leave" with their families. I immediately got in touch, calling on the one who was staying in London and leaving my book behind for Dr. Black and his wife to read. I and Mary had lunch with them and their daughter in town and afterwards, during term time, they came down to lunch in the country with us. Doctor Black was especially surprised to see how beautifully made Mary was and astonished to hear I was 'like a young woman again', only weighing 7 stone 8 lbs. [*A surviving letter confirms this meeting.*] "Nevertheless," said he, "I expect Mary is really your last and final effort." He was greatly mistaken.

Dr. Smalley, who had operated on me, came with his wife to stay for a weekend after they had read the book. They too were most surprised at my youthfulness and strength. Though I had been warned I might grow very stout after that operation, I was now slighter, more agile and full of untiring energy. He too agreed Mary was above the average in speech and independence. They both loved John. The Doctor warned both parents he would need a great deal of care still, and building up, especially his blood, and advised Glucose D and Calcium lata. This I bought for the lad and his wound healed quickly. Within six weeks of leaving hospital he was able to put trousers on and walk without a limp. But he still looked very pale and I felt he ought to have a blood test. "There is something wrong," I said to my husband. "He tires so."

So his father obtained permission for the lad to be put through the Medical Test of the R.A.F. To our great surprise and joy the lad passed A.1. He had had to go before a heart specialist, especially called in, in the afternoon, as one of the R.A.F. doctors evidently had a doubt; but the father, knowing the irregularity of his own heart, said "Oh no, my dear, it's not the boy's heart because of his burns, but in this he takes after me. You know how often they have tried to plough me, and the lad's passed! It's great! I asked about his leg muscles; of course he needs exercising up. They advise it every morning."

To the boy he said, "My lad, before breakfast you're to run round this Park, and do some exercises with a stick. Then a cold bath. You will have to start work now you're fit. No more lying about; real hard work. There is a Kitchener exam, and the King's Scholarship to Cranwell. We will see if you can pass as a gentleman before we work you." He was accepted for both, but was told he would have to take his Higher Certificate first. [*From the context, I think my mother means matriculation, or passing in five subjects in his School Certificate, including English and Mathematics.*] As he was only 16 he could be considered again the following year.

I pleaded for him not to be sent back to what I termed "that hateful school", but that he should have individual attention, especially as he was so backward. I hoped in this way to give him more motherly care, little realising what it would lead to. So the lad began working six weeks after being on his back or on crutches for eleven months, without a seaside change or real holiday. His paleness seemed to get almost transparent at times. His hands were often purple. I begged for a blood test; I had no faith in R.A.F. Doctors, who had condemned my husband as unfit, and were passing my son as fit. But my husband relied on the RAF medical. "You don't realise, my dear, it's the very stiffest examination to pass. Even I, my dear, who as you know can do everything, can't pass it, and John has." "Yes," I said, "yet John can't dig as you can. He suddenly tires. Just can't do it." My husband thought he just needed exercise to strengthen his muscles. But he also wanted him to "get on with his work and pass this examination." "What hope! In three months!" "No matter, it will give him an idea of what to do the second time."

The lad tried his best to work, Lotty helping him. Together they worked and exercised. She sent to Germany for her black running shorts and gym shoes. She was so strong and full of action; he, so feeble. He never, to the end, was able to put "muscle" into it, for more than two or three efforts. He would lope round the Park like a slow old wolf. He never seemed to go full out. This inability to do anything with energy, of which both his parents had so much, made us feel dreadfully irritable with the lad. We failed to understand why he could not do what he used to do, especially as he had been passed A.1. We would argue and become bitter with ourselves. The lad never answered back, and that annoyed even more.

He confided to his new Head Tutor whom he greatly liked "I can't work some days. My mind at times becomes just a blank. I cannot think, far less do." This master on many occasions advised the father to "leave the lad alone". "He is a good lad," he would say. But the father suffered under the delusion the lad was not caring or trying, especially as now and again John showed real brilliance. "He's got it in him, why can't he concentrate and get it out?" he would ask. Why? Why? No one knew or guessed, or tried to think.

Lotty, after six months in England, had to return to Germany, and as John was able to go to Town with his father, I carried on alone.

The third child and stress for all

It was John who asked for Susan, our second girl. He kept on saying to me privately: "Mother dear, do have a second before it's too late. You both will be old when Mary grows up. Give her a companion, someone of her own age." I remembered his remark to the Maternity Nurse soon after Mary was born. On being told by me that he had a little sister, he had said: "Oh nurse, how tragic!" "Tragic, John?" "Yes I have grown up alone and now she, poor wee mite, will be alone too." "But she will have you." "No, Nurse. I might be her Father and my parents her grandparents. When she is 18 I will be married with a family of my own, aged 34."

So I asked, "Were you very lonely then, John?" "At times dreadfully, Mother dear. You need your own age to understand your point of view, or you feel you do. Dad only appears to remember his good points when a youth and yet I feel he could not have been perfect as he expects me always to be. Oh, don't you understand, Mother? You must have someone who not only will feel the feelings of youth, but will act and enjoy it with you. Dad, because of his heart, is old for his age. He does not want to play golf with me, swim with me or play tennis. It's always 'amuse yourself''. And Mary, she will find the same. Do you realise you will be nearing 65 and Dad 70? I will look after the children if you will have two, but not a lonely one, Mother dear."

But my husband would not have it; and when he heard God had stepped in and I was to have another child, he was furious. He said and did all the unkind things he could think of to show his disgust. He said he would hate it. But John and Mary, when asked if they would like a baby brother or sister, were thrilled. So I said to my husband that I would do nothing to prevent it, but would not encourage it as I did in Mary's case. I cooked for the household, did the laundry and looked after Mary all day. Mary would never leave my side; even watched my bath, patting me and saying: "When I grow big will I have a big tum-tum too for my baby?" "Yes, dear," I replied. "I think you're lovely, Mum-mum." It's a good thing someone does, I thought. John, when he came home at night, always drew up the sofa and saw that I put up my feet." I expect you have quite forgotten to do this in the day, Mother dear," he would say.

One morning I felt I would love a quiet lunch in town with my man, instead of an interrupted one, feeding a small baby and attending to the needs of others. Something I had not cooked; to get away if only for a day. My husband was not too pleased with life that evening so I decided to wait till the morning. It was a glorious sunny morn. Mary, being dressed early, was out in the garden before breakfast with her father. I came down dressed in my best, never expecting a refusal. "Dear," I said, "I would so love to come up to town with you and John in the car and lunch with you at some quiet place. Mary and I can play in Hyde Park till it's time to come home." "If you think I am going to be seen with a woman of your size, you're d … well mistaken. I won't even allow you to come up in the car." My surprise at this attack made me burst into tears. Mary, the wee mite, ran to her father and thumped her small hands on his legs. "Bad, bad Dad, to make my Mummy cry."

I went in. John too had been watching from the open bathroom window. I called the family to breakfast, but felt too upset to eat, and started to arrange the flowers. John came out to me. "Mother," he said, "will you do me a favour?" "What's that, my son?" "Come and have lunch with me in town." "I have no money," I said. "But I have," said John. "Enough for us." "Dad does not want me to use the car with him in it." "Never mind. Come by 'bus. Here's 2/6d, and I will meet you at Selfridges. You could then go to the Park and I will see you come home in the car. Come to my Tutor's. Dad would never dare say anything there."

So I decided to go, catching a bus just in time to meet John, taking Mary with me. His politeness and thought were for me. We had a nice little lunch. John persuaded me to rest in the Rest Room as he and Mary had shopping to do. He had his photo taken with Mary as a surprise. Not wishing to take further advantage of his great kindness, I refused the offer of a cinema and said I would prefer to return to the Park, not having a sou. At 5.00 p.m. I walked down to where I knew my husband left his car and got in the back seat with Mary. When he arrived he looked but never said a word, and drove the car off to meet John. The lad was waiting. "Oh you got in, did you, Mother dear." Then the father spoke. "Did you know your mother was here?" "Yes, Dad. I invited her to lunch with me." Silence.

John seemed to get better, certainly until the failure of his first examination. We were not upset, as after all he had had less than three months to work for it, but to him it was a bitter disappointment. The effort to pass had taken so much out of him. He had had to pass in five subjects, all new work, and one a quite new subject to him. He failed badly in Mathematics, a subject he hated. John was really good at drawing but was never given a lesson to prepare him for his examination, nor time to practise at it. Still he passed in that. His father disliked this art and regarded it as useless; he himself had a mathematical brain and never could see the lad's difficulty in that subject. There were dreadful heart-breaking rows for poor John. He would be set algebra or arithmetic to do in the car after his day's work, by his father. He was tired. So tired he could not even try to concentrate and they would both arrive home exhausted; his father for having lost his temper, and John for trying to contain his and disappointment at himself.

Once or twice John would fail to come in to the house, calling "How's Mother dear and Mary" as he usually did, but would slip away to the woods to hide his tears until he felt he had hold of himself again to return to a bitterly sarcastic meal, and after it to try and work again in the dining-room with the supper things pushed to the side; and listening through the thin walls to his father, resting in the sitting-room easy chair, cursing his wife for such a brainless son who would not even try. In fairness to John he did try, but was so stale, tired of this work, work, work and no play, no companionship, but work, work, work.

The more I pleaded the more it seemed to goad the father on in his dreadful keenness for his son to do well in the subjects the father had found easy, and in his desire for the lad to be what he wished him to be and not what this artistic and mechanically minded lad wished to be. I was never allowed to forget that my brothers had proved failures to their mother, who had had such hopes of them, although my husband had nephews also as great, if not greater, failures on his side. How anxious the lad was to succeed for his father, to prove to his father that he had been worthwhile. So often when Mary was quoted as 'clever' and likely to get on – a wonderful child – poor John would say: "And what about me? Aren't I going to succeed for you too?" Yet he never got any encouraging or comforting answer – just silence.

Even on the day before an examination he would be cross-questioned if it happened to be the mathematics exam. When he returned he had to show all his answers and working, and go through it again with the result that the lad would go up in a blue funk and return to continue the other subjects with the hopeless feeling of, "Well, Dad says I have failed again in Arithmetic, so I have failed the examination," knowing that he had only taken the minimum amount of subjects.

He grew more and more relaxed. His morning exercises were more easy-going, his bath became warmer. He seemed to slack in everything. "It is exercise he needs," was the next cry, and this time from me. "There is too much stooping over these books. Out of doors, my lad. Join a club and get some games and to know other boys." To my husband I said "I feel something must be done. Can't you get him games or join a club for him? I begin to wonder if we were wise after all to have taken him away from school, but I hated him to go back to that one, and you felt he was too old to start at another."

The lad took it into his own hands without saying a word to either parent or asking for a penny. He never asked for money, knowing full well it would raise a storm. He had been told too often of the expense he was; and that was also given to him as the reason I had to labour so, when he tried to plead for more help to be given me. I, too, never went to a cinema, nor, poor lad, did he, unless a friend or aunt took him, which amounted to about three times in a year. His pride was too great to beg for his own pleasure; instead he saved out of his lunch money and joined a local tradesmen's club for Rugger, run by a parson for 10/6d. a year. He even bought his boots and Rugger outfit, his colours, sweater, stockings and shorts. How proud he was of it. He would wear them in the morning to run in. Neither of us ever asked him what he had to pay for them or how he managed to do so. I saw the bill for the boots paid for and was astonished at the price. I did offer to pay for those but he assured me he had had a birthday and Christmas tip. I had given him a £1 as I always did; his father 10/-, and yet with the subscription it would hardly cover the cost of the outfit. He only played when a game was near enough for him to cycle to, or go by bus, within his savings. He never asked for his fares and his father only once went with him by car. The father remarked to me after that match that the lad played well and showed keenness, but was too light for those very heavy men.

Once he tried to arrange to learn to box at a very low class club. The greedy manager, seeing he was a gentleman and getting his address, wrote in the worst English a misspelt letter to the father asking for £3. 3. 0. John had said nothing. I, on being shown the letter, asked his father to go round and see if the lad boxed during his lunch hour. His father went and was horrified at the lowness of the place and the utter rogues and forbade his son to go again or to any such place to learn to box. He might get damaged for life. "I thought," said John, "it might make me more alert. I seem so slack. I can't pull myself together. I thought this might make me use my wits in self-defence."

I noticed during the second season that the Rugger was gradually dropped, and asked the reason why. "They are too heavy for me!" the lad owned. "To try and bike a long distance, play and bike back, I find too much." I agreed. Nevertheless he always wore his colours for his daily early morning run before breakfast.

Black-eyed Susan arrives

John had had a week sleeping in town, to be especially coached in his homework by an aunt. His examination was due in ten days' time. He had asked if he could return home the same day the maternity nurse was to arrive, as he said he felt rather interested in the babe and would like to be near to hand. He was told he would have to have a camp-bed in his father's already small room, which Mary was also to share. The new cook-general would have his room and Nurse and the new babe to be in the spare room; I in a small but sunny dressing-room next to Nurse's room. A kindly neighbour, hearing of John's wish, offered to give him a bedroom to sleep in. John was greatly relieved. He was to have all his meals, etc., at home and so did not feel cut off or 'not wanted'.

It happened to be the maid's evening out. I had bathed and put Mary to bed as usual and then went down to cook the supper. Nurse was collecting my things and came down to supper, remarking to me, "You're doing all the work." "Yes," said the father, "She is far too well and I expect she will keep us waiting a few weeks to add to the expense." Nurse smiled. She was the same Nurse who had attended Mary's arrival, and so knew the family well. The same Doctor was also to attend me. I had had a fierce battle over that. I hated being mauled about by strange men. Dr. Moss knew me and I trusted and liked him. He was the kindest, most thoughtful and the gentlest Doctor I had ever had. He always knew where to put his hands and at the right time. John had stuck up for me over this, his father wanting a local man who, he thought, would 'do the trick' for a £5 note. I told my doctor of my fears that my husband would call in a local man. He said he would write to him and reduce his fees. He also recommended a very good local man, should he not be able to come in time or if a doctor was needed for the baby or household afterwards.

That evening my husband remarked to me: "I had extraordinary luck; I won the Doctor's fees today by backing an outsider. I suppose you put that down to the mercy of your 'Light' again," sarcastically. "Yes I do," I replied, "especially as you've spent all you've won on buying and exchanging cars this year. Three cars in nine months!" "My money." "Well, I hope you'll keep this to pay my Doctor promptly and not keep him waiting. He's been goodness itself to me."

We all went to bed; John to the house next door, the others to our rooms. I was waiting up for the maid when I picked up my daily paper and wondered if there was a message for me that night. I read: "Come unto me all ye that labour and are heavy laden, and I will give you rest." 'Well,' I thought, 'I had better have a final tidy round,' which I did, getting to bed at 11.15 p.m. I slept till 12.15 and then woke, realising things were about to start, and so woke my husband. "Come and move Mary, I believe things are about to start and I would hate her to hear and see me in pain." "Well, call Nurse; I cannot do it alone." I called Nurse. "All right, dear, I will get up."

I went back to bed. The pains grew worse. No one had moved. I again went and roused the father and nurse. "Please come and move Mary." The nurse got up and dressed. The pains continued to quicken; I went out on the wee landing and into the bathroom, anywhere away from the peacefully sleeping babe. I had warned Mary, when the new baby came she would be sleeping with her Dad for a little while as Mummy had to go to bed alone. Nurse would take care of the new baby and another Nanny would come to care for Mary in the day time and take her out. "All right," said Mary, "I will be good." She was – marvellously.

At last, after what seemed ages to me but was only thirty minutes, the nurse and father came to move the crib and sleeping babe. She woke and cried out: "Daddy, Daddy, has the new baby come?" much to the surprise of the nurse. At ten past one the father and nurse having just finished moving the entire furniture of the wee room round so as to get my bed in the position the nurse wanted it to be, and I begged them to inform the Doctor. I was still walking about. "What, already, dear?" said Nurse. "Yes, now. You forget he has a long way to come." "Are you feeling as badly as that?" I leaned my head against the mantelpiece by the newly kindled fire. "Well, you had better go and telephone," the nurse told the father.

As he slammed the front door, I uttered a cry: "Quick, quick, Nurse, it's here and I can't move." The nurse pushed the unfinished bed towards me just in time; the babe was born on the very edge, a dark black hairy mass. "A girl," said Nurse, "and as unlike Mary as it's possible for a sister to be." "Her cot is not ready." "She'll have to wait at the foot of her mother's bed." I sat up and looked at my babe – "What a mess." "Lie down and let me attend to you first." I was having such strong after pains I begged her not to touch me but to wait for the Doctor. "I'll faint. It's awful; worse than anything I've ever experienced."

My husband, after twenty minutes, knocked at the door. "I've phoned," he said. "We've got the baby." "Good God. You were in a hurry," he said to me through the closed door. "Within an hour of calling me." I lay in pain and moaned in agony.

The Doctor came. Voices downstairs. "Not needed now," said the father. "Quick, quick, Nurse, don't let him send the man away!" The Nurse ran to the door. "Come at once, Doctor, you're wanted." The

Doctor came, smiling placidly. "He would not let me in – had put the chain up – I guessed something like this would happen and yet I was quick – an hour and twenty minutes." "An hour and forty," I said. My husband, thinking there was no hurry, had walked to the railway station, instead of phoning from next door. The Doctor gave me an injection, the pain died down, peace reigned.

"Well, you have a little black-a-moor this time". She was hairy, all down her back, face, ears, black down and such quantities of long black hair on her head. Black lashes and black eyebrows and a dark red yellow skin. *[My mother told me later that my father had phoned a relative "Black-eyed Susan has arrived" – hence her name.]* Not the fair, delicate pink and white of little Mary. Her temperament, too, was completely different to Mary's. She bellowed into life – no need to smack her – and continued to bellow and protest strongly. Nurse said never had she such a tiresome wee soul to train to sleep. She yelled, it seemed, all night long. From 2.00 am to 4.00 or 5.00, sometimes from 12.00 till 3.00 or even later. I used to lie and hear the nurse through the wall getting so furious with the babe. She used to scold her, and put her on her face. The strong wee soul raised her head, turned it and continued. She was only quiet if loved. If Nurse took her in her bed she would sleep sweetly; put her back in her cot, even with a hot bottle and cosily wrapped, she would yell. It had to be the human touch. She would stop as soon as picked up; as soon as she heard a caressing voice, as if the wee soul felt she had been starved of love as her mother had been during her coming. "I often find these babies," said Nurse, "who have caused a family strain by their coming, tiresome to train."

Susan kept it up until she was over a year, night after night. It was most curious she was only good and then really very, very good, sleeping well and longer than Mary in the morning, if her father was out of the house. When I had her away by myself she was good and peaceful; returned to the fold – war. So it proved it was nothing to do with food. She was strong, a much stronger-looking child than Mary; much more hungry. She always has been and remains active, a fighter, a protester, a wee creature of passion. She loves and loves to be loved with might and strength. Mary, the summer child, was always sweetly gentle. Susan, the winter child, vigorous, passionate, forceful. Both possessed immense affection and power to express their love, but they are two different types. Strong characters, but summer and winter.

Mary could never be cold. She burst into tears if hurt – summer rains. Susan, even as a wee baby, could express coldness and contempt by her expressions. Her face is the most expressive and makes full use of her beautiful dark eyes. Not the gentle pools of clear blue of Mary's. They could never flash scorn only reflect joy and gladness, and sparkle with pleasure, else they wept. Susan never wept tears to make her eyes red and swollen. She roared; she fought and scorned to cry soft tears. She never cried if hurt, but up and at it again with even greater vigour. Mary spoke really well at 18 months; Susan did not, but she walked at a year, had all her teeth, could knock Mary over and pull her down when 18 months old. She fought for her rights – hitting, biting and pulling if need be, and took her punishment but clung on till she got what she meant to have.

There was no need for her to speak. She could express herself by look or carry a chair and climb and get what she wanted. She rode Mary's tricycle at 18 months alone. It had cost her many a fall but she did it, and without help. People would look at her and say, "Of course she is pretty." "I can't see it," I said. "Yes," said her father, "she is a good looking child."

Really he was very proud of her, although he always showed his love to gentle Mary and pretended he had little use for Susan. Susan adored him. She always had from the start made eyes at him, held out her wee hand to him, but it was Mary who had the toys until the mother and friends protested at the cruel unfairness of bringing one child home a toy and none for the other. "Perhaps," I said, "that may be the cause of Susan fighting Mary so. When you're not here it's peace. When you're here it's war by day and restless crying by night. Be fair. She is here now. Don't kill her natural deep love for you. If the two girls become friends, and not jealous of your affection, perhaps Susan may be gentle Mary's protector, even though she is younger, in later years." "What rot you talk," said my husband, but he improved after the great shock shortly to take place.

Now back to the struggles of a struggling house, trying to get over my great tiredness after the birth of Susan. "You're so much more tired than after the birth of Mary," remarked Nurse. "I am. I have done more. I am too tired to feed Susan. She is too hungry. Give her a bottle. There's that free sample of 'Cow and Gate' that will do." It did do. Susan became a bottle-fed baby.

John's second effort to pass his examination was interrupted by the birth of Susan, the baby he wished his mother to have for the sake of companionship to Mary. He felt a sort of responsibility for her. How could he be expected to settle down to serious work when his mother was sick upstairs and the house all upside down, squalling babies and nurses and maids all muddled together in a small four bedroom house, the bedrooms the size of dressing rooms. Where was there peace and quiet? The nursery was the sitting room, which was also the general room and John's study. He had no bedroom in the house, as he slept at a neighbour's house. Still no excuses were given by him for his failure nor was there forgiveness. His father was very bitterly disappointed. Maths again was the subject he failed in. Passed all the rest. This was really not surprising as he brought his questions back and his scribbled answers for his father to see after each exam, and these were gone into with a feeling of failure far into the night, although the lad had to be up next morning to take another subject and have more words during the drive to town, where the exams were held. I too felt so depressed and distressed to listen to it all and unable to stop it – shut off in my bed with only the thin walls between and my cries of "Do let the lad go to bed" unheeded. "You must get away," said Nurse. "I will pack you up and see you off before I go."

Physically I had healed well. Mentally I was still overwrought. I did not feel nearly as fresh as after Mary, although Susan had been only an hour in coming. But the pains of the after-birth and all the worry I had, not understanding John's seeming slackness and yet seeing his great love for both his parents and trying to keep the peace between father and son, and between myself and my husband's anger at the unwanted babe; I felt utterly exhausted, unable to battle with the house and cooking, as well as the babies.

The Nurse and Doctor persuaded me I needed a change, to get out of the rut and toil. Leave the men to cope for themselves; John was old enough to be under his father's care. A sister-in-law offered to have me and the two babies for a fortnight by the sea, and then an invitation came from Grandmother to extend the visit and go to her for a fortnight as well, and have the baby christened at Easter. Grandmother was asked to be a godparent, John also but he would not decide. He said he must see what was expected of him first and then would think it over after he himself had been confirmed. What Church was the babe to be brought up in? He himself was 'low'. I said I did not mind the kind of worship as long as it was real and the most helpful to that particular nature. After all, worship, meaning 'church service' is only a form to get us out of ourselves into the correct atmosphere to receive the word of God and for us to be able to send 'our cries' over to Him. "I believe in prayer," I told my son, "no matter if you're kneeling, sitting, standing; the thing is to throw your mind out of yourself into God and His sphere. The Church that helps you most to do that calmly and reverently is the Church to go to for worship and service.

"Well," said the lad, "let me be confirmed first and have a week to think it over." And so I left him to be confirmed alone. I knew if I was at home his father would make some excuse for not attending and somehow I longed for my husband to attend his son's confirmation. Perhaps a greater understanding would come between the two – who knows?

Nurse helped me pack up and saw me into the car with the two babies and luggage, three weeks to the day after Susan's birth. The father, after depositing the family and luggage, returned home to John. A charlady was to tidy up after them. John had to get up and get the tea and breakfast. The father cooked whatever supper the woman had left prepared for them, while John worked at maths.

While away I thought how greatly I would like to be with the lad at his confirmation, even if I could go for the day, but there were the babies to see to, and besides I realised I had no money. Squaring up the housekeeping bills, run up while I was in bed, and paying off the maid I had to get in to cook, and a daily woman to look after Mary, and the Maternity Nurse, I was very much up against it. In fact, so much so that it took me 18 months to recover from my debts. I felt I could not ask my husband as he had not wanted the babe and still was rather brutal about it. I must bear this myself and because of my faith in the Light I took heart.

To my son I wrote a letter telling him of my joy and belief and knowledge of the Great Love who understands all men's efforts and to whom I would pray that he might also know of that Great Love and Comforter. I told him prayer was the means of communicating, no matter how quietly and simply spoken, so long as it was in earnest and concentrated. I said I had such faith in him, my son, that I wished him to be Godfather to the new baby. So he agreed.

Meantime, how were John and his father faring? There was no buffer now I was away, no relaxation from each other, except when they were both at work, and John's work absorbed most of his time. His father was his own master and could tarry at the Club. The father, when he joined his wife for a week-end, owned the lad got on his nerves. I understood as I had felt it too. To me John looked and seemed so ill, minus some blood corpuscles or something I used to say, but his father would never agree because the lad had passed the Royal Air Force test. To him the lad seemed "so damned slack" – modern youth. "He never seems able to try and put beef into it." John would never own he felt ill, perhaps because he had been like this too long. He never lost his temper with his parents' chiding. He was silent and his silence annoyed.

One morning I received a letter from my husband telling me he had lost his temper completely and flogged the boy as he had never flogged anyone before. The boy looked ghastly and it frightened the father and made him desist. The lad never told me and I never spoke of it to him. "I have promised him a car and long holidays if he passes," said the father, "and he seems to be working better for it now."

Later, he wrote and asked me to look for rooms as he felt they must have two months' holiday after this exam – John's third effort, with no holidays between. Would I come up and see if I could 'let' the house. I decided to return after the christening at Easter. Grandmother invited the father and John down for the Easter weekend. Susan Ann was christened on Easter Day. A beautiful christening. Grandmother, who was also godmother, had decorated the font, made a beautiful cake and invited all the relations who could come. She also received some beautiful silver christening presents, so very many more and more beautiful than either Mary's or John's. John said he would be godfather and went to early Holy Communion first. So very, very in earnest. "I have no money to get her a present yet," he said to me, "but I should so like to give her a napkin ring, a thing she will use every day, and I will save for it." Curiously he and Mary had them as presents, but Susan Ann had a silver sugar basin, milk jug and a mug. *[I think the photo in the frontispiece was taken on this occasion and paid for by Granny. It was always in my mother's house.]*

On our return home I became worried over John, yet I never realised it was tiredness. I thought it was lack of outdoor sport and again spoke to my husband. I paid the fee for him to join a local tennis club and also for a dozen lessons of half an hour at a time, fixed for every Friday evening after he came home from work. He had to change quickly and cycle there and back, a distance of three miles each way, and return to a very late cold supper. His father also arranged tennis lessons, but in town, or rather at Ealing. The lad took his things up in the morning, had a forty minutes' lesson with a really celebrated Wimbledon player, and he had to catch the tube to meet his father again en route for home or see himself home by train or 'bus. Both tiring. He found these lessons too hard. He only went up, with much pressing, for five of them and no matter what was said, refused to go up for his sixth, much to his father's great disappointment. Did the boy feel it too much and not wish to alarm? His rugger that winter he chucked completely.

"They are too much for me," he told me and I, remembering what my husband had said the one time he did go and see the boy play, I said nothing more. Yet he was keen to be a sportsman. His desire was so very great that he used to cut out pictures of experts and notes on tuition from the daily papers and carefully paste them in an exercise book with odd notes, not only of rugger but of drilling exercises, etc., etc., and even in these books he could not help drawing most neatly, as if to scale, wireless diagrams for both long and short wave sets. All his spare money, all his Christmas and birthday wishes were for money to buy odd wireless parts. His room was always having the electric light altered for effect and experiment to different parts of the room. His walls were a mass of 1/- blue diagrams for wireless sets as well as aeroplanes. He would pin up for a day or so a cutting he wished to remember of a hint either on wireless, rugger or electricity or atmosphere. He was never given spare time to really get his nose into it, for if he stayed in his room long it was "John, come out and garden", or if the weather was too bad and he went in, it was "What about your work. Surely you have not finished?" He would pack his spare wireless parts up when he went for even a short holiday with his parents, or take a bundle of magazines in the hopes of being allowed to indulge in his keenest hobby.

Debts piled up. Try as I would I found I could not square my overdraft at the Bank. I had borrowed on the money left in trust for me by my mother to try and pay for the extra expenses of Susan's arrival had caused, rather than ask my husband for it, knowing he would again blame me for having the babe. He had had the money. God had seen to that, not only by luck of racing, but also from his father who had died just before Susan's birth, leaving him a legacy. So in desperation I asked him and got what I expected, a cursing.

He could never see that because of my faith in the "Light" and my vivid vision I would have to accept what was sent to me bravely. My explanation of my faith and trust in God only made him more and more furious and bitter. He could be so very bitter and hurt me so very much by his words, more than he realised. John and I hid our worries and fears because of his bitterness and lack of understanding and sympathy. He expected sympathy always to be readily given to him. Perhaps because he knew he could obtain it, he would threaten to "chuck them", or "drive a man to drink" or it "upset his heart". For days he would make home life miserable by sulking over "the hardships of his lot", never realising he was only spoken to because things were becoming too worrying for me to bear alone. How could I pay? My house-keeping money was expected to pay when "I want my shoes mended", or to have the trousers and suits cleaned for both men. It had to stretch to the extras needed for a baby and small Mary; the coal and coke bills, laundry while I lay ill in bed; Insurance stamps, wages, note-paper, stamps for all the family; the large chemist bill which included shaving soap and Gillette blades; and the large household food bills the temporary servants had run up while I was in bed, with no extra help of money to pay for it. My allowance was £16 a month.

My temper grew shorter and shorter; no help or sympathy from the man I wanted it from. Tears would stream down my face as I hastily peeled the potatoes to cook the evening meal for the men, after I had hurriedly bathed and fed the babies and put them to bed. They were now both good babies for going to sleep. I never had time to stand for any nonsense such as rocking or sitting by their bedsides, and leaving doors open. Bed meant sleep. However, Susan with her first teeth started bad nights again. The babies used to sleep alone. When I got up to attend to Susan it so disturbed poor father that he insisted on a cheap nurse girl, but he never offered to pay for her, and so although this girl was a help to me physically, she added to my mental worries over debts. My bank found out my money was in trust and so they would not allow me an overdraft any longer, putting it right for themselves by taking my house-keeping allowance. Of course this action piled up outside debts.

John needed his holiday badly. He seemed at breaking point. Seeing his parents' worries and hearing of them from both sides hardly helped him with his studies. The father said he meant to have his holiday at any price. The rooms ordered in the spring at the sea seemed impossible. I wrote and cancelled them. Instead I wrote to my husband's people, explaining my need for help.

I realised the foolishness of trying to stay on in our present house. The rent and taxes were too high, and especially now the family had increased. I wrote to my Trustees and asked if I could sell out and buy a house. I would not mind if it could ease the home tension by our living 'rent free' or even let my husband pay me a small rental, say £30 or £40. The house would be mine and held in trust. This they refused to do. Talk, yes, talk and talk, and worry me more and more by saying I was only exaggerating the family's difficulties. If my husband wanted money, let him borrow it from his rich relations. He would not, or could not. I thought would not, and said so. Still no help. I prayed and prayed. My temper became shorter. I was weary by day and too weary by night to sleep. I became over-tired and one morning I woke to find my voice had gone, and my body refused to get up even if I wished. My legs refused to hold me. A Doctor was sent for, and a woman to help the young inexperienced girl care for the babies and run the house. The holiday had to come. A sister-in-law wrote and offered her home for six weeks. A fortnight for me and the babies and nurse girl, free of charge, and then a month with John and my husband, joining us and sharing the household expenses. John had to sleep out but was to meal with us all. This kind offer so refreshed me that I was able to pull myself together and visited all the local estate agents to try and 'let' the house, even if it only covered the rent and rates while we were on holiday. I was fortunate enough to let for two months which would just cover our rent and rates, but not our living expenses. So I wrote to the seaside place and took the rooms already ordered for the second month. These rooms had been re-let for the first, this suiting our changed plans.

Although I joined the local tennis club for him at his aunt's, John would never fix up any games. His cousins found him far from keen. I started to play myself and was very disappointed to see what little interest the lad had. He seemed even too slack to pick up the balls, and when we moved to our rooms he requested to be let off all games, just enjoy a "slack" by the sea. Here again, although he could swim and dive really well, he would just stand about in the water looking blue with cold. He would play a little with the younger set but so quietly compared with what he used to do. He did not greatly care for girls although they liked him. He preferred men of his father's age. They used to ask him out alone and always found him good company. They used to say to his father that the boy was a lad you could talk to. An understanding, sympathetic lad with high ideals and sensitive feelings, and yet his father never found him so. Children loved the boy for the same reasons.

And I, when most worried, would confide in him for I knew he would give me his attention, love and sympathy; although he often pointed out his father's point of view, he seemed to realise mine as well. He was very, very fond of his father, and often said to me: "Oh, let the old chap have his way, Mother dear. He has a much more difficult nature as his thoughts are for himself first and foremost, let us be calm. You old darling," and he would kiss me. "You know you both are dears; you both love each other, but you are both such fools at seeing the other's point of view. You're both right and you're both wrong, as you forget how differently you are made, and temperament can be so upsetting, and so blindly selfish. Make it unselfish because of your love. I'll help. Don't ask for pocket money for me. I can manage. Old Pop, since Lotty left us, has forgotten to give me any, but still I would rather you had more. You spend nothing on yourself; any fool can see that but Dad. It's funny how he can't see how much you spend and give up to us all. Poor old mother. Cheer up," and he would throw his arms round me, giving me one of his hard, crushing kisses.

I could not make love to my husband and then ask him for money. To me it would be sacrilege. Mine was love for love's sake. My friends and relations, especially the women folk, knew of my power and often said: "Why don't you get it out of him? He loves you. Do urge him." "I can't," I would reply. "You see I love him too, and I am no street girl to bargain myself. I would feel a slut. It can't be done." It never was done. Often I was going to tell him of some worry, when he would intercept me, and then I would have to shut down that worry as I could not spoil our love by worries of any kind, especially money ones. My love for him I kept as some holy thing, quite separate. Something apart – alone – not of this world.

Now and again John would talk of his work, and the hopelessness of his Maths. His father wanted him to take this exam for the 3rd time – "Pray, John," I would say. "There is nothing in this world that can help you but prayer. But you must first be earnest, first 'get a connection'.

You know, dear, like your wireless set. It will not work if there is even a little something wrong. Get it all set for a right connection. Get the mood. The concentration of prayer. That's why I do not go much to church. I cannot concentrate at church. Someone bawls too loudly, or coughs or fidgets. I am back on earth. 'My set' is howling. So try alone in your room. Read your Bible at a place that will help you best and then concentrate. Get your mind thrown up – off – out of you. It's difficult. It may take time but it will come. Especially if your desire is there. God is Love, that I know having seen the 'Light', and I would let you read about what I have seen only your father thinks I am mad, and has begged me not to. So all I can do is to tell you, especially as I feel it is not my time to make my book public yet, as I feel I must do and am meant to do later on. Believe me when I say Mary would not have been born if I had not seen the 'Light' of Love beyond Understanding. Susan, too, would not have come if I had not feared to disobey what I had been told to do. I believe in what I have seen. I trust it. 'Spite all things'. Do the same, my lad."

I knew he did heed my words, as I always saw after that talk, when tidying his room, the small blue Bible by his bedside and out of curiosity I carefully noted each day that the marker was moved. I had first given him this Bible when he went to Guys Hospital as the best comforter I could think of when alone.

That third examination was doomed to be a failure too. Baby Susan started teething. She fretted by day and yelled by night. Joan, the nurse girl, wished to leave. Her mother was ill, seriously, and she felt she ought to go back and care for her and look after her house when she returned from hospital, to which I agreed. After all I would like my daughter to do the same.

Financial worries were getting more and more pressing. My husband too was very worried over his expenditure and although I did not know it then, he was also worried that he might be out of a job. His temper towards his household was nearly unbearable – unapproachable to either son or mother – all locked in that small four-walled house in an atmosphere of pent-up silent pain – antagonistic to each other's feelings because each thinks only to spare the other more worry, kept silent of their own, being bound to each and all by LOVE.

We all three did things unbeknown to each other to try and help. The father visited numerous firms to look for a job in case he lost the one he was in, which he never did. All so unnecessary were his worries. His job grew and grew and with it the financial side as well as interest. John wrote to more clubs and wrote to various advertisements to improve his English and his physical and mental worries.

I wrote to various relations and friends in the hopes of borrowing a large enough sum to pay off all my numerous little debts and so be only owing to one man, and ease my conscience by paying that one interest. I even visited moneylenders and was horrified at the interest they asked, but all replied they needed my husband as a guarantor and that I knew was useless to ask as he preferred little bills and no interest. My next endeavour was to change houses. I would answer and write to many agencies but the weekends came and he refused to motor round the country, having motored up to town five days in the week. So I could only inspect those near at hand. I found one that they all seemed to love, especially John and Mary. It was large enough to give the children room to move in without being too rambling. It had for me and the children a homely atmosphere. How delighted Mary was to find she could open the doors herself instead of the new fashioned houses with handles so out of a child's reach that she felt imprisoned once the door was shut. The garden too was big and wild and yet well planned – something in it always to do and not feel lonely, not a small neat square patch with the air of 'finished'.

One day my husband visited it with his sister, as Susan was not too well. She thought it too large. The cheapness never appealed to her, nor how dry and well built. She poured cold water on it to her brother. Off they went to see another house, as small as the one we were living in. My husband went with her to the agent, unknown to me, and made an offer for a house he had never consulted me on or his children. When they returned I was too upset for words that the man I regarded as my helpmate could do such a thing; treat me as such a chattel. I wept for the hurt of it. Even John was aroused and stood by me. As for Mary, she could not bear the house with doors she could not open when I had found one where she could. The battle took days, weeks to fight. Luckily one of my husband's brothers sided with my wearied and hurt self and persuaded him that his wife and children had to live in the house; while he only slept in it.

Still the gilt of the gingerbread had been broken, to be still more spoiled by my own uncle who felt, as a solicitor to one of my trustees, he should have first been consulted. He and my aunt thought I would be lonely. Putney or Barnes would be better, never thinking how much I loved gardening. It was a cheaper hobby than shop-gazing, at the frocks I would have to have if I went nearer town for bridge-parties and all the more expensive forms of amusement. The battle raged on. I fell ill again. Not only did I wake one morning to find my voice had left me, but my legs seemed paralysed. I felt too utterly weary and just could not get up. For the second time a woman had to be sent for to mind me and Mary while the men went up to town. The Doctor was sent for. I had a subnormal temperature and very low blood pressure. He said rest and a tonic; bed and no more worries.

But the worries came. Two days later, as my voice was returning, I felt able to move again. But I was still in bed, when my husband returned with flu which developed into bronchial pneumonia. Up I had to get. He took my bed in the small room. I and Mary moved out. Unfortunately the next day was John's first day for his third effort at his examination. He too had a very heavy cold, but nevertheless went up in blinding fog. At 6.00 am he rose as with no car he had to take a cross-country journey by train. He came home looking so wretched, his cough and cold so heavy that I took his temperature, but like me he was subnormal. His father insisted the lad had to get up and go next day. The Doctor, who called twice that day, warned me my husband should not to be excited or crossed as he was really ill and his heart in a nervous state. John and I consulted downstairs and left it that if the lad felt no better he was not to go. "Poor old Dad would be so upset."

The next early morning again was dense fog and drizzle; the lad swore he felt fit and went. He had by bad luck one examination at 9.00 am and the next not till late afternoon, so he did not arrive back till 9.00 p.m. The father anxiously waited to cross question him on his day's work. The lad stuck to it for nearly ten days.

One evening I noticed on his return how dreadfully pale and transparent he seemed. I asked where he had had lunch. "I did not have anything all day," was the reply. "What?" I exclaimed in horror. "No money," was the calm reply. I went up to my husband. "Has John not had his money this month?" "No. I could only give him enough for a week. I meant to give him some more." I was too wrathful to speak, knowing he was ill. A cheque was found which he signed, and John was sent out again in the cold to cash it at a public house, the shops being shut. What chance had the sick and starved lad? Of course he failed, but only in the subject he knew he would – Maths. He passed with Honours in History.

The day drew near for moving house. My husband feared he would get ill again. It always took him longer to pull himself up. He could do nothing to help but sat about as an invalid. John and I worked. I had a very kind neighbour who realised the size of the task with two babies and a sick man and no help, and who found me a young lad of 16 for 8/- a week. At least he could help move and scrub and clean. I wrote to Joan and asked if she could come back even for a few days to look after the babies. I bought myself a car licence and learnt to drive my husband's new car.

We finally moved. It went so smoothly that even my quarrelsome husband was astonished and thanked me for having seen to things so quietly, quickly and comfortably. The house was warm. It lent itself to comfort. The children too were all delighted. Everything fitted as I knew it would. Everything looked much better, although old, as it could be properly seen and we had picked up on our travels some beautiful things. Grandmother had written and invited the family down for Christmas weekend. This fitted in well. We moved on 20th December; the workmen left, carpets down, even books, vases and pictures were up on 22nd December. Joan went back to her home and the house-boy to his sister's for Christmas, and the family to Devon. There we enjoyed Christmas as it should be enjoyed, a time made over to the children; Christmas trees, decorations, turkey, plum pudding and numerous presents. We returned home happy and thankful to a new, clean and tidy house which seemed to welcome us as we stepped into the hall.

John's final efforts

Back to work for John; only a week's 'leave'. The cold and his cough had re-occurred, unfortunately for him, on Christmas Day, perhaps due to the cold journey down in the back seat. He was unable to quite throw it off all that winter. I pleaded for a day in bed for the lad; as I knew how much good such a rest did for me, but no, the father was firm. He did not think the lad bad enough; only that he could not miss a day's study. He was to be rushed into a new examination; an easier examination, he thought it would be for the boy, quite forgetting new subjects, new periods of history; new plays and verses for English to learn would not make it easier – all to be done within nine weeks. Less than that really, as the father and tutor wasted a week in discussing whether this would be wise. The father won.

The weather kept bitterly cold; nevertheless John was made to get up and go for his early morning run as usual. The father had had the tennis court re-dug, much to my wrath as unnecessary expense. John was made to stamp it in again at 6.45 to 7.00 am those cold and frosty damp mornings. I protested. "Better by far send the lad for a run. He is blue with cold, stamping in a slow but steady line." More arguments; whichever of us reached the lad first. It took some chivvying to get him up those mornings. He was tired and yet we never realised it. We just failed to understand how down he was. His teeth ached. He had them attended to and yet they ached again. He complained he could not sleep at night.

He came back one morning from his early morning run, after having done some stamping, and meeting me just going to my bath, said: "Mother, I got winded and passed out this morning." "Where?" I said. "Oh, just at the corner of the road." "Are you all right now?" "Yes, quite." "You had better not run any more these fearfully cold mornings." He went to his room. I went back to mine to tell my husband. "John said he passed out this morning. He'd better stay at home today." "He can't possibly with the exams so near. I will see him." After breakfast I again asked the lad if he was OK. "Yes, quite," he said. The father ruled he had to go up as usual. I helped the lad on with his coat and muffles and came out to the car to see he was warm. A few days later he complained of cold. He was told he was old enough to take care of himself, but never allowed to do it.

Susan decided to cut four teeth at once, and became most difficult. My husband remembered he had never registered her. Now he was in a new district and had to go out of his way to do so. He was fined and asked if she had been vaccinated. He did not know. He returned to ask me. "Yes once, but it never took." "It's got to be done again and at once. No more fines for the wretched kid." The Doctor was sent for and decided in spite of teething and owing to her age, now nearly 14 months, it had better be done at once. It took; very, very badly. I was up nearly all night. The house echoed with her yells, poor babe. The wrath of the father was great. How could he work if he could not sleep? Even patient John complained. "It's either my teeth, or Susan, that keeps me awake."

The Saturday before his examination his tooth was so painful he pleaded with me to get his father to motor him to a dentist. My usual dentist did not work on a Saturday. I rang up a friend who recommended one. I begged my husband who was digging in the garden to break the unwritten law "no car at the weekends", and motor John. "Let him bike." "He can't. He is in such pain." Many curses, he went in ill-temper to get ready. I saw them off. I could not go because I had no nursemaid, only the house-boy, and Susan was not at all well. I felt so wearied that I realised I must have another woman in the house and wrote to the German girl, Lotty, to either come over and help me again, or send some other girl. Lotty decided to come if I could wait till after her father's birthday. Could I wait? I felt not, but I said I would. It was decided that Lotty would come on 28th March, sailing on the 27th March.

Monday arrived. John's examination. His tooth had had a bad abscess, and he was injected as the dentist was not authorised to give gas. The injection made the lad feel and look quite overcome. His father received a shock on seeing the lad come out to him. He was very thankful he had driven him in the car instead of making him cycle. I got the lad tea and hot bottles and lit a fire in the sitting room so that he could be quiet. He was very low all day, and yet neither parent thought of sending for a doctor. I knew I owed the doctor bills for attendance to the family, including the father's illness, but never for John for nearly 18 months and I felt too ashamed to meet the man, and so John suffered.

The sister-in-law who was so against the house wrote and asked if she could come up to stay. The father insisted. He wished her to see how nice it all was. Meantime a sister of mine, whose husband had left her penniless, was staying with us for a week. She was astonished at how seriously the father took the examination. He would talk to the lad going up in the car what to do and what not to do. Coming home, long rehearsals of what he had done. One evening, towards the end, the father and son returned, both looking ill. The lad burst into the kitchen crying: "Mother, Mother, Dad says I have failed, failed again in my Maths! Oh, Mother! Mother!" I calmed him, and went into the sitting room to find his sister had given her brother a whisky and soda. He also was quite overcome. "Why get so excited before you know the real answer?" More wrath. "Well, next time John shall not have an examination to do, with you in the house causing him all this worry. He will live in town with my sister whom he loves." "And who is going to pay?" asked Papa.

"I will write to her and fix it," I said. His sister agreed it was impossible in such an atmosphere. The father was too keen, too anxious. It might be himself who had failed.

John heard the result during a week when he was home on 'leave'. Yes, he had failed. Passed with honours in English, History, but only scraped through Latin and failed hopelessly in Mathematics. He now, poor lad, was quite dejected. He seemed unable to read or garden, or interest himself at all. He sat in a stupor. He would not eat. I was very worried. I told my husband that he must have more than a week's leave. "He has to go in for it again by June." "Well, he won't get anything if you don't give him a second week in the spring sunshine. He is done in, I tell you," I said.

It took such a lot to make an impression on this very determined man. So keen, so dreadfully keen, and so disappointed that he could not see the lad's greater disappointment and hopelessness. They could not speak. The father was so sarcastic and I had to get angry to arouse the lad, otherwise he would sit and stare in front of him, doing nothing, feeling and looking hopelessly dejected. I chased him into the garden, into the lovely sun, for the days were warm and spring-like. His father set him garden tasks to do. The lad failed to do them and was cursed.

He tried. Once, after a cursing he said to me: "Yes, I must try in this to please the old man but I am so weak." "It's because your muscles are not used to it," I said. "You have studied so hard and not done any muscular work." Together, when I could escape the housework, we toiled, I pushing the barrow, he raking feebly. "I am fed up with the garden. I wish we could get a day off from the babies and go to a cinema." "I wish we could," I said. "I have no money. Has Dad given you any?" "No, and I am not going to ask him. I have failed." "Well, I shall," I said. "He owes it to me for feeding you. Why should he have it all his own way?" "He says he too goes without his luncheon." "Have you?" I asked. "Oh, I've cut mine down to 5d. At Lyons. I am trying to pay off a bill." "What bill?" "Mother, I am old enough to have secrets of my own." "Well," I said, "your aunt comes next week; perhaps she will take you out."

She did, once, to a local cinema. On being asked what she thought of John's condition, she could not see much difference in him and backed the father, her brother, in thinking it was all my fancy and love for my son. So back to work John went, after only two short weeks at home. On the same day the house-boy stayed in bed with a sore throat. My sister-in-law decided to go to town for three days and return on Thursday evening with the men. So I had now babies, sick nursing and meals to get and cook single-handed.

The National Health Service had just started, so I asked the boy who his panel Doctor was and he mentioned the son of my own doctor. *[My mother is confused here. There were some improvements in 1935 to the existing service of 'panel doctors' who for low but certain fees, looked after those families with an earner who had paid National Insurance.]* I phoned him to come. He came in the afternoon. Finding the Medical Insurance Card unsigned, he said: "I really think you are too far away and suggest you get a more local doctor to attend to you." "Who can you suggest?" I asked. "I don't know of anyone but I think it is too far for us." He went. I thought, 'That's because the bill has never been paid – over eighteen months' old. Another bill to fall on me as my man will say impossible. What am I to do?'

I told my husband on his return. "Well, get another doctor. John, tomorrow when you are out for your run, you can look for one." Both parents had forgotten in the worry of their own troubles his, and had hunted him out of bed as usual. John never reminded them; perhaps he too had forgotten, suffering from tooth-ache and general deep dejection. I, noticing this, tried hard to cheer him that evening. "Well, how are things going?" "Oh, Maths, Maths, Latin, Maths." "What, no other subjects?" "No. I am only to take the ones I failed in. It's awful." I went to my husband. "The lad will go mad if you don't give him a subject he likes as a break. His face is terribly tragic." "All right. I will speak to the Tutor at the end of the week. A week won't hurt him."

Next morning John noticed a doctor's name plate on a cottage gate and went in and asked him to call. Breakfast over; the men went off to work. I was also suffering with bad tooth-ache, and found a woman to mind the babies while I went to have them out. It was decided that I was to have four or five out and two new plates. The dentist told me that when he was drilling John's tooth it seemed too much for him. "Oh," I said, "he has had it out now; it had to be done on a Saturday." That evening I asked the lad about it. "Did it make you feel faint?" "No," he replied, "not more than usual. I often feel faint."

No doctor came to the house that day. John was blamed. "But I did order him," he declared. "Well," I said, "the boy's temperature is 103. I have put him on slops. I am so nervous with the children. I have forbidden him out of bed and have to do everything for him. You must go for another doctor, that's all." Supper. After supper I saw John studying in the hall. He looked so ill it gave me a shock. "What is it, John?" I asked. He got up and came to me. "Mother, it's Maths, Maths, Maths." "Dear," I said, "what do you really want to be? Your aunt told your father you were not keen on being a doctor." "I feel I can't keep this up, Mother."

His look cut me to the heart. I said nothing but went straight to my husband who was sitting by the fire in the sitting-room and pleaded on my knees that these exams might cease and that the lad might follow his own interest in wireless and electricity, especially as the man who took our former house so liked the lad that he had offered him 25/- a week to learn the job and come with him in making electrical and mechanical machines needed in businesses. He had again been to the boy's father, offering 35/- for the lad because he liked the lad's personality so much. But his father had said no. He wished him to be a doctor in the R.A.F. Now I pleaded and for all my love and begging was told the lad had to pass this examination and could not be let off. "But why Maths for a Doctor?" "It would mean so much to say he had it," the father replied. "Supposing this man found the lad was no good after all, and turned him out? Besides, for moral grounds I do not wish it." This man had a wife and two children and yet was living openly with another woman. My husband felt this would not set his son a good example, and that if he was tempted after marriage, he might fail to keep his marriage vows because his 'boss' whom he admired had not. It would not be fair to so young a lad. "Have you seen the Tutor to get a change of subject?" "Not yet, but I will."

John had written to join some Territorial as a "Tommy" at Camberley. When his father heard he made him write and resign and he promised to try and get him a commission. Thursday arrived. The sister-in-law returned. The house-boy was better but not up. Two doctors had arrived; I took the first. The explanation was they only visited the cottages every other day for that district.

The aunt was full of praise for another brother's son of the same age as John who had just passed as an army cadet to Woolwich. "How proud his parents were of him. Our son, etc. etc." "I wish," said the father, "I could say the same." I saw my son wince and anger filled my heart. The other lad had not had a father to badger him. His father was in India, he lived with his mother in England. He was allowed to get on with it unhampered with family cares such as John shared, and also no such great set-back as the burns.

Friday. Lotty arrived and greeted John with: "Why, John, you're just the same as when you came out of hospital. I did expect you to look stronger. Same pale John." He laughed and kissed her. "Yes, the same boy and so I can kiss you still." I laughed. We were all seeing the babies to bed in Lotty's room. Mary had remembered her, to her joy. She had brought presents for them all and gave John a German record. "Where is my gramophone?" "I lent it to Thomas," I said. "I will get it for you tomorrow. He is asleep."

I never did. Seven people, the new doctor and his family, came to tea and in the effort of attending to everything with John's help it was forgotten. I had asked them as I felt I had done no entertaining for this sister-in-law; not even been out with her, and she was the sister who had been so very good and kind to me and the family, having us all in the summer after Susan's birth. My husband wished the party to be put off as he thought it would be too much with the house-boy still in bed, and no one to open the front door. "I can do that," said John. "After all I am a sort of butler to this establishment as it is. It won't be anything out of the way," and he smiled his whimsical smile. "And a jolly good job too, my lad," said his father.

That evening, when the men returned from work, John looked very dog-beaten. "What's up? What's been the trouble?" I asked, as he helped me get the supper ready. "Oh, I don't know. I cannot do anything right. I went to sleep in the car instead of learning some Latin words. Dad had told me to get on with my work. I meant to but fell asleep, and he was furious. I am useless as usual. He and Aunt are talking of my uselessness now in the drawing-room, so I came to help you." Sure enough during supper and after supper, in front of Lotty, we had all to listen again to the wonderful achievements of John's cousin, who in reality never had such a hard life as John had had, nor had he been expected to be as unselfish as John was expected to be by both his parents. Even his room was not his own. John had to clear out; John give up. Because although he hated doing so, he did it with such good grace, which made him most loveable.

Death – foretold but not foreseen

Saturday came and with it a letter for John by the first post. He visited me in my bedroom. The letter was from the Adjutant of the Territorial saying he had been granted a commission and would he call on the Colonel on Monday. How delighted the lad was. "At last, Mother, I am going to be allowed to do a man's job. It was jolly decent of Dad to see about it for me. I never dared hope I would get it. You will see I will be worthy of it. Make you proud yet, Mother darling." "I know you will, my son. It's just what you want; it will make all the difference to you."

It was a happy day for him, although a busy one. The Doctor called to see the house-boy and said he could get up. John was in the hall telephoning when the doctor went. The doctor looked towards the lad as I had spoken to the doctor, a stranger, about my son and his father's desire for him to be a doctor on day in the R.A.F. The doctor had also a son struggling to pass the same examination, but he kept failing in English. "Now," said the doctor, "if your lad failed in English instead of Mathematics, you might have a worry, but mathematics is not going to be of much use to him as a Doctor. Why not take another subject?" "My husband shone in mathematics and wants the lad to pass in all he did. He is set on it and cannot see the boy's difficulties." "Extraordinary."

A second tea party was arranged for that afternoon and went off with great success, excepting for one instance. John had taken great pains to ... look extremely neat and well groomed. His dark navy suit was well brushed and pressed; but he was worried over his shoes. His black ones were not back from the menders. ... They had not been returned as the shoe mender wanted his 5/6d. first. I could not pay for them, having no money at all, nor would my husband produce it. John also was without pocket money. There they had to be left until the end of the month. ... I went up to the loft to find an old pair of my husband's dancing pumps. Luckily they fitted.

At tea, it was perhaps the after effect of getting up the heavy attic ladder for me, and helping me move all the trunks that caused the lad to feel it was an effort to wait on the guests at tea and run for more hot water, etc. There were pots of Indian and China tea. When I appealed to him, he replied: "Oh, give them what you have got; it does not matter if it is Indian or China." The guests being in the room it made me feel very awkward.

After tea he just sat in the drawing-room and quietly talked if spoken to, but made no effort to show off the garden, as he would have done if feeling well. When the guests had gone he asked me for half a glass of sherry. Getting up to help me, he nearly fell. "Why, John, what's up? You cannot walk properly." "I don't know, Mother. I feel dizzy. I cannot have a head for drink. I cannot think how Dad manages it. I won't be able to." ... "Go and sit," I said. "No thank you. Aunt and Dad are discussing me again; my ill manners at tea. I am sorry, Mother, but I felt fearfully fagged." I noticed his blue lips. "You certainly look white; go and sit."

He went. His father offered him some more sherry. He took it but remained still and quiet. After supper he looked better for it. So much so that his father noticed it. "John, you're looking better," he said. "How do you find him, Lotty?" "Just the same. Not a bit different; certainly no stronger." "By the way, Mother, you never got my gramophone from Thomas." "I will go." "Oh, leave it now. He is sure to be asleep, but try and think of it tomorrow." So it was left. Soon after we all retired to bed. As John said "Good-night" to me on the landing, he asked: "Shall we go to Early Service tomorrow, Mother?" "Right, dear, if Susan gives me a good night. Mind you call me in time as I am so tired I shall be asleep."

Susan was terrible that night. I woke at 12.45 and did not sleep again until 5.15 am. She slept in the Day Nursery alone, as she was such a disturber of the peace. I had to get out of bed again and again, much to the wrath of the father, who slept in a single bed beside mine. When at last we did get to sleep we were awakened at 6.00 am by small Mary, who always insisted on crawling into my bed on waking. She had been sleeping with the German girl, who did not like to change the little one's habit so soon. Mary was quiet and we slept again until the child became restless at 7.15 am.

"Oh dear, how dreadfully tired I am," I yawned. "I feel too tired to move, but suppose I have to get up to get the tea." I had quite forgotten I had promised John to go to church. Just as I had finished speaking John came in with the early morning tea, dressed in his dressing gown, and must have heard my remark to my husband. His face had its usual sweet smile, as he set the tray down by his father's side-table. He had to pass the double window and the wallpaper was green. The father had chosen that as he regarded my visions as imagination, and John laughingly had said, "Oh, let Pop have his choice, mother dear". "Well done, my son," said his father, as the lad drew the window curtains. "You had an awful night, Mother. I heard Susan." "Yes, awful. I am so weary."

He came over and kissed me and Mary, and quietly went out of the room. His father, excepting for saying "Well done, my son," was too tired to take notice of the lad. John never reminded me that I had promised to go with him to Early Service; instead he quietly changed into his sports gear. The Rugby colours of the Club he had joined off his own bat; the colours he was so very, very proud of. He always washed them himself. This morning they were especially cleaned in Lotty's honour; white gym shoes, his red and blue striped stockings, navy shorts and red and blue jersey. His hair well brushed, he went off for his early morning run.

It was a bright, cold and frosty morning. He did not usually go for a run on a Sunday. Whether he was feeling fitter or wished to get fitter, so as to be more prepared to become an Officer in the Territorial Army – his interview was for Monday – or it may have been having got up to go to Early Service and seeing how tired I was, he thought he would please both parents best by a run off his own initiative instead of being hunted into it. No one will know. No one saw him start off. It must have been about 7.30 am. His father, also seeing how really played out I looked, got up and went down to cook the breakfast. I, still in my dressing gown, got up to show Lotty how to dress the babies.

Mary had been dressed. Susan was still being dressed. I went to the airing cupboard to get a garment for Susan when I heard the car in the drive. I looked out of the landing window and saw my husband with a stranger struggling to get John out, a limp form that lay wedged between the seats on the floor of the car. I rushed down. Still in my night-gown, dressing gown and bare feet. "What's happened? Poor John. I will see to him. Give him to me." I pushed my husband out of the way. "You can't lift him with your heart. You telephone for a doctor." Taking my son by the shoulders I succeeded in heaving him out of the car, with the help of the strange man. He turned out to be a former lorry driver at my husband's last R.A.F station. Curious that he should be the man to live in the nearest cottage to the common, where John had pitched down, within 200 yards of his own home. For all the lad knew he was still running. His hands were clenched and arms doubled in running attitude. As the woman who found him had described, he had just pitched forward on his face.

His face, when I saw him, was pale, ivory white, with purple lips and purple blotches behind his ears and on his forehead where it seemed he had hit the ground. I was anxious to lay him on the hall lounge chair, but his father was nervous Mary might see him and insisted he should be carried up the narrow back stairs and laid on his own bed. So up the back stairs we went. The Sergeant with his feet, I with the weight of his body in my arms. His arm round my neck and held by my hand, my other arm under his seat.

The stairs were dreadfully steep and narrow. We could only go up single file. Somehow I seemed to have all his dead weight, which with a great effort I helped myself to support by resting the weight of his body from one knee to the other, as we climbed the stairs. At the narrow twisting corner the Sergeant saw the weight was too much for me, and let go of the feet to try to get round and support me. I nearly fell and with great effort heaved the body up nearer to myself, and I swear to this day that that extra heave shook something in the lad. Perhaps the wee spark of life, as he opened his eyes and seeing me smiled. And I, so delighted to see life, cried: "It's all right, John, my lad. Mother has got you now. All will be well with you. Don't worry."

As the smile departed from his lips I saw and felt the flicker of life go.

The Sergeant said, "Steady, madam, steady," for his concern was more with me than the lad I bore alone in my arms for that moment.

Aftermath

We bore him up to his room and laid him on his bed, undid his neckband but could feel no pulse. I ran for hot water bottles and found the water in the tap was cold; called my sister-in-law to put on the kettles; then to the nursery to warn the German girl to keep the children in the nursery by giving them their breakfast which luckily the father had cooked. Back to John. Still cold, still blue. I collected more blankets from my sister-in-law's bed and ran to hasten the hot bottles. Back again to the Sergeant and John to find my husband trying to force whisky down the closed lips. "Have you phoned the Doctor?" "No. I thought you would." "How could I and carry John? Go now at once." "Who shall I call?" "The nearest."

We had the same man John had opened the door to on Saturday. I took a looking-glass and held it to the boy's mouth and nose. Not the faintest sign of breath. I heard an inward voice say to me, 'You with your faith can cure the lad by respiration and prayer, but think of what you felt and saw when you were like this.' I sat above the lad and pumped, and as I pumped he began to draw in deep breath. 'Think, think,' said the voice, 'what you are doing. He has passed into the Light. Would you, who so long to go there too, and are now so discontent, would you call him, your Loved One, back from happiness, to pass through the pain you went through on your return; to come again to more troubles of this earth when you know he will be blessed and happy? Think, think.'

I thought and stopped. He stopped breathing too. I pumped; he again commenced to breathe in.

The father returned. "What's that? Is he alive?" "No, not yet." I stopped again to show. "Keep on," the father said. I kept on but without prayer; instead I thought back on this young lad's life of toil and thought of what greater toil was still ahead should he revive like I had done. Would he ever be happy again, having seen the 'Greatest Love Beyond Understanding'? Had not he reached his reward to be allowed to go and live in the Happiness and work his way on to final Heaven. The place of all great hearts' desire, where only the strivers go? Had not Jesus come and lived and was He not ready to die the hardest death so as to return straight to the Seventh Heaven instead of to the lesser heavens, or Paradise, there to wait for our misdeeds to be born again and return to make one more perfect. Yes, let him go to the God he knew and which I saw that he knew by the way he had reverently prayed at Susan's christening and at Holy Communion. No need to fear for John now. If he returned he might not win again so good a place with so strong a Light in his soul a second time, as I felt he had now. He had prepared for his earthly service of Holy Communion, his prayer book still open, and now had been accepted into the Heavenly Communion. No priest could have prepared him better than he would prepare himself, being such a truly conscientious lad. God had heard his cries of despair and had taken him to Comfort and Heal as no earthly parent realised how great the lad's desire to succeed was.

"Try the glass as I pump," I said to the anxious father. The glass was dry. It was cold air coming in and out. He still was cold. Chilled right through as he had been left out there to lie when life was ebbing away on that cold and frosty morning. As another hurried by to be in time for her earthly communion service, he had gone to his Maker's arms to enter His soul and in time to be One with Him in the great never ending Light of Salvation. The Light that had no turning, no winking; one steady, pure white Light radiating Love beyond Understanding. Such I knew. Had not I been prepared by this same Light to be able to bear a grief which my own mother knew would otherwise be too great for me to bear? Had not the Heavens and Souls seen me bravely standing up to my beliefs amongst a critical earthly audience? Prepared to take gossip of any kind for the sake of the God in whom I only believed in then. I did not know Him before that, but because of my faith and courage I was rewarded by this vision which to me meant so much and gave such a steadying Comfort and forethought to the minutest detail. Now my greatest earthly grief was upon me. How could I grieve as others did, knowing my son had not died but merely shed his earthly body like a caterpillar to blossom like a butterfly to greater joys and greater knowledge. He lived and would become one of those joyful laughing voices echoing with happiness as those souls' voices did whose duty it was to bring me back to earth after my vision, even to teasing me, as I thought then.

Now I realised they had not teased me. I had come back to England to my baby son, my only son. Such was Fate. To be accepted. Lived bravely. Would my turn be next?

At last the doctor came. He too seemed surprised at the deep drawing in of breath. I stopped while he listened to the dead heart, so tired of Life and its effort. The doctor then took the looking glass and tried the mouth and nose. No result. At the father's request he injected camphor of a kind in the lad's arm and tried to revive the heart himself. No sound came, not even the drawing in of air I had achieved.

"I will show you," I said, taking my lad's head in my lap I pressed his lungs with my great soft hands. Again he seemed to draw in deep breaths. Still the heart did not answer. "No, I am afraid it's no use," said the doctor and expressed his sympathy to us.

I did not weep; the memory of the Light was still before my eyes. I turned to my husband, who not knowing the Light as I knew It, was overcome, and gave him all my attention, and what relief I could from the trials of attending to all the things that had to be attended to now.

Then I remembered my babies – Mary the intelligent little girl of 3 3/4 years. I thanked God that John, as Godfather, had already spoken to the child of God. One night, as the babies were getting into bed, John and his father had come in to say goodnight, only six weeks ago. "It is time, Mother," said John in his serious voice, "Mary said her prayers and knew something of God." "Oh no," said the father, "she is far too young." And Mary, full of curiosity, said: "Yes, tell me, John. I want to know who is God". The father left the room. "You tell her, John," I said, and this is how he told her:

"God, Mary, is a most wonderful person; so wonderful we can't think of any other person being like Him. He made us and He loves us, even more than Daddy and Mummy and I love you. He can hear us whenever we speak to Him, and He can see us and talk to us. You need never be frightened. You can hear God talking to you inside. You know the little voice that says inside you 'that was my good Mary' or 'that's bad; you must not do that'?" "Oh yes, I know," said Mary all keenness. "I have heard Him. Where does He live?"

"He lives in a place so beautiful and so happy we can only think of it as the blue sky and call it 'In Heaven'. When you hear people calling the church 'God's House' you will know that is wrong. It's God's school. That's why you have got to be good and quiet and do what other people do, like you will have to do when you go to a school to learn to read and write. God's schoolmaster is called the Padre or Vicar. He is the man who tells you what to do like a schoolmaster and tries to teach you about God." "Yes," said Mary, "and what are those stones in the garden of God's school?"

"Those stones are put there by different people in memory of God's favourite flowers. When a person tells you your great friend is dead, Mary, you will know it is not so. God has given us butterflies. We are like caterpillars now, and will leave our bodies behind, crawl out of them into a chrysalis, rest a while in a different world, then leave those bodies behind and awaken like a happy butterfly to glory in the Sun. Tomorrow we will look for caterpillars and their earthly world, the leaf they work on, and put them in a glass jar for you to see how they make their own coffin to rest in till it is time to wake like butterflies."

Each morning when time allowed, Mary would run to John and watch him dress and chat about the wonders of God and Heaven. Now I realised no one must tell Mary of John's passing except as the lad would have wished her to know, so I left the doctor, my husband and the Sergeant, and went to the night nursery where I found my husband's sister and

Lotty with Susan. Mary was in the Day Nursery sitting on the floor in a ray of sunlight.

"Mary, darling," I said, "John has gone to God." "Oh Mummy," was the smiling, happy reply, "how happy he will be now." "Yes" I agreed as I kissed the upturned fair face. Mary sprang up and ran to her toy cupboard. She and John had collected green caterpillars and put them in a 2 lb. jam jar with a cabbage leaf. They had become chrysalises and now as the small child opened the cupboard door the jar was full of fluttering white butterflies. Mother and daughter took them to the window – no word spoken. The pierced lid was lifted and the butterflies soared to Heaven in the sunlight. A dove cooed in the garden hedge. Peace fell on them as mother and child kissed again.

[Another early snapshot memory I have is of being in my mother's arms, watching the white butterflies fly out of the window. I did not know its significance till the 1950s, when my mother first showed me her book.]

Regrets

The Sergeant was thanked and departed. The doctor left; the grown-up members of the family went down to breakfast which the father had been cooking when first told of his son's collapse.

At breakfast I remembered another breakfast while my first-born was arriving. The dreadful shock in the morning newspapers over the Battle of Jutland. I had read that my husband's ship had sunk with all on board, quite falsely put in. I had struggled to swallow something for the sake of the 'babe to be' and failed; and now I and everyone else were quietly eating boiled eggs, toast and butter, and tea when that babe who had grown to be my comforter passed on. Astonishing? No. I had not known of the Light before, and this knowledge I realised was my Comforter, my strength to carry on so quietly.

After breakfast my husband wished to phone to various friends and relations. He asked me to let my people and the aunt and uncle with whom we had had such a disagreement over the house know. For John's sake things must be forgotten and forgiven. I begged them not to come over as I was seeing to everything and could manage. Nevertheless they very kindly did come with a practical gift in the shape of a bottle of brandy.

My husband had already phoned the really kind late neighbours, who had had John. They were people who did much and talked little. John had loved them dearly, especially the dear kind hearted wife. They arrived within ten minutes, before the uncle and aunt. This relieved me, as I wished to be left undisturbed to 'lay out' my own son before the police, with the hearse, came to fetch him away, since an inquest was necessary as he had fallen in a public highway. I brought a basin of warm water and Eau de Cologne, bathed his face and washed his spotless hands; his ears, feet and nails were beautifully kept.

"Well done, John, my boy," I spoke aloud to him, caring for him as if he were a new born child. "You're so perfect there is nothing for your mother to do. In fact, dear lad, you shame her, for your feet are much better cared for than my own old hands," and I caressed them. The friend came in to see if she could help but realised her greatest help would be to keep others away. Dear, true friend indeed.

After everyone had departed my husband came up to fetch me down, and he seemed annoyed and worried at seeing me bathing my son's feet. "Oh, leave him, dear. I hate to see you touching him. You might cut him." "As if I would. Besides there is no need. You might help me to get him out of his tight sports sweater. I wish to dress him in clean pyjamas." Together we lifted the lad. He was a weight. Even heavier, it seemed, than when I carried him up the stairs. Both were astonished how warm he had become. He who was so cold was now warmed by five hot bottles and blankets and the camphor injection. In moving him he gurgled. "What's that?" his father asked, alarmed. "Perhaps the whisky you poured down his throat," I replied. He was changed and a clean sheet laid over him. "Now do come down," begged my husband.

I went and was taken to the drawing room where there was a tray of empty wine glasses and one full one left for me. "I honestly can't swallow it," I said, though I took a sip for my husband's sake. An egg I could eat, but this burnt and seemed to me profane. John had never liked to see me even take a glass of sherry. I had never had anything at home for the lad to see until after Susan was born when, with the weariness of coping with two children, the house and cooking, I had made it a habit to take a wine-glass of some kind of pick-me-up, so as to be able to seem refreshed, sweet and of good cheer when the men returned. John would always try to wrestle the glass away until towards the latter end he too pleaded for a refresher in the form of a glass of sherry or ginger wine. Poor lad, how weary he must have been.

Not being able to sit still, I wandered back to my son and sat beside him on his bed. I then noticed on his bedside table my present to him when he first went to Guy's Hospital. The Bible I had given him was opened as if just read, St. Matthew VII 7, marked: "Ask and it shall be given you; seek, and ye shall find; knock, and it shall be opened unto you." And on his chair neatly folded was his best suit ready for the Church Service we were to attend.

I felt his pockets and found in his vest pocket, with his pocket-book, two small paper booklets of prayers. I was astonished. I had never realised how devout he was. These prayers looked well used and a leaf here and there turned down, evidently the ones he liked best; all praying for Heaven, to be and do God's desire. The letter telling him of his commission was there. What a lift up in prestige that had given him. Also a bill for two guineas from 'I will and I can', British Institute of Practical Psychology Limited. What a worry that must have been to him, and how he cut down his lunch to pay this great bill. He who would never ask for money. How else was he going to pay for that, I wondered, as I got up to collect his sports clothes. These I would burn. He loved them so. They were his – no one but he should wear them. I took them out into the garden and made a bonfire. They burnt right to ashes. I collected them to put on the garden he had tended of the house which he had described so recently to me as "the best we have ever had".

My husband came out. He needed me. He felt dazed and upset. Although his sister was there he seemed so lonely in his sorrow. I took his arm and tried to cheer him. As we entered the house the policemen arrived. They wanted a statement from us both. They had found out the name of the woman cycling to Early Service who was the first to see the lad lying on the edge of the common, still breathing. She thought he was merely winded, turned him over on his back and cycled on. At the top of the road she met another woman who lived at the cottage by the cross roads, and told her to watch and see if the young fellow recovered as she did not wish to be late for her Church Service. The other woman said she would go down and found him, as she thought, already dead. She tried to massage his heart and then left him to go to the nearest cottage for help. It happened to be this ex-Sergeant's, who had so recently served with my husband in his last Station, and so knew the lad. We did not know this man lived there. The Sergeant sent his son to tell my husband, who left the breakfast he was cooking and went at once with the car, unbeknown to me.

As the police finished hearing this story the back door bell rang. I went. There was the Sergeant; he explained he was so distressed he had to return to ask if the lad might have lived if they had gone and fetched a doctor on the spot instead of trying to move the lad, as the father insisted. "Don't tell my husband your feelings," I warned him, "but your feeling life was still there comforts me, as I too felt he died in my arms as we were trying to carry him upstairs. That's why I spoke to the lad as I did. I saw sudden consciousness and life flicker away with a glad tired smile. Come up to his room, my husband may find us here." I took him up and there told this stranger, this man, the story of my Light, the reason of the babies' coming, sent by the request of my mother, to comfort us when this my baby, a boy, was wanted. I sent the man away, as I hoped, comforted.

The undertakers arrived. We saw our son depart to be taken to a small white tiled mortuary on the hills looking west, behind which the sun set, surrounded by heather and pines – nature the boy loved. Sleep for three days and then to arise again like Christ did. I went back to my lad's room and seeing his little Bible still open where he last left it took it up and read all through the chapter. I then opened his private drawer, which during his life he had forbidden anyone to look at, and knew he would prefer me to be the first to see his treasures. I found a packet of letters neatly piled in a corner. The first was a letter from the 'Superman' in answer to his enquiry as to where he could train to get fit.

I looked further and found they were nearly all answers to his enquiries as to how he could better himself in the body by exercise and outdoor sports, and mentally and spiritually. What a silent struggle it revealed. What great desire to prove the success his parents longed for him to be and which he so echoed. How quietly and bravely borne. I next found a thick small book, so neatly kept, of which he had carefully numbered the pages, making an index at the back of it. In it he had written the names, addresses and telephone numbers of various clubs, under their allotted pages for their sports, all within reach of either his home or Tutor's. The first page was devoted to the Head Office of the Associations. I found he had written to many sports and football clubs and had cut the advertisements out to write to the 'Anglo-Japanese Judo'.

He had made carefully and neatly written notes. *[These were on the bus fares it would cost to get to and from each. She gave the example of the four fares needed to get to and from Sunningdale to Cranford: total 2/8d.]*

How pathetic never to have had the pocket money to go; and still more pathetic on the back page of this secret book of longing was a collection of mathematical formulae – things his father would ask of him at all times of the day … Poor John, how he hated it and how, as this book showed, he must have felt it …

His despair and wretchedness must have been great indeed, and yet he tried to pull himself up. He had cut out an advertisement from the Personal Column of the *Daily Telegraph*:

> "INFERIORITY COMPLEX – Write for FREE BOOK "I can and I will"
> British Institute of Practical Psychology Ltd."

And had answered it, asking for help. They sent him down a book and also a paper of questions he had to answer, which they replied and corrected and then sent him a second, and a bill for £2. 2. 0. What a shock to the lad! He had understood that they offered 'free' advice. How was he to pay this? He certainly could not go on with this desire to regain his confidence at such a price. How his parents might laugh at him and be so annoyed, especially his father who always said "Rot" when warned by both masters and mother not to give the lad an inferiority complex, but to leave him alone to his studies, a thing impossible to his father's nature … And his mother? How could he ask her? He knew she was working, washing, striving and worrying to keep up with bills that overcrowded and overcame her. No. It was just another thing he had to endure silently. The firm wrote letters of appeal to touch and so hurt his feelings, knowing as he did he could not pay £2. 2. 0. even if he would. If it had not advertised 'free advice', he would never have written in the first place. Now he must suffer silently for his foolishness in believing it, and do without a mid-day meal.

The other letters he received were from the Clubs which proved too expensive or too far afield for the £2 a month which he was supposed to get regularly, but some months he did not get it except in daily driblets out of which he had to pay for his luncheons, teas, if any, odd sweets, bus and tube fares, papers and cigarettes. He smoked very seldom but now and again. All the boys at his Tutors were older than he was and smoked; naturally he, at 17 to 18, would like to keep up with them. Often his father chided him for not making friends and going out to lunch with other fellows, little thinking it was owing to the expense. How could he afford to go to places the other lads went to, his money being so much less? He started to take the 'Superman' regularly and secretly at 9d. a week in his endeavour to get fit. He took it, I found, for nine weeks.

I went through his large wooden box of electrical and wireless fittings and numerous books on the subject. Except for a few puzzles and a rug-making set belonging to the days when he had to lie abed for eleven weary months owing to his bad burns, there was nothing else but his paint boxes and pastels.

How glad I now was that I had kept and framed his beautifully coloured drawings and pastel works of flowers, etc. A nearly finished wireless set, so exceptionally neat. All his work was neat and tidy. Clever hands. A frog, cut open and pinned out to reveal all its inside on a piece of wax, floated in methylated spirits. He had only had a blunt pen-knife and a pair of small nail scissors and yet no trace of a spot of blood. What a good doctor he would have made, both sympathetically and with those clever hands. Yet perhaps God wanted him for greater work. Such a great quiet patient soul could not die. I never felt that. He was still near me, unseen but near. Yet how I blamed myself for having been so over-tired with the babies and house and cooking, that I had thrust this very sensitive and striving, unselfish spirit on to a man like my husband. I should have known how little my man cared to be worried by other people's worry, and how little he understood of another's outlook, always thinking of his own heart and health and worries, and being so childlike in his cries to me for help. How this son, like myself, would do anything rather than add to that man's worries, for he loved him very dearly. 'Poor old Pop!' If I had to go to strangers rather than to my man when worried beyond being able to keep things to myself when I felt I had to 'overflow or burst', he, my son, had preferred 'to burst'.

What did all these letters, books, etc., point to? Short meals, thought I, starvation diet while working hard and training hard on a system already undermined by his fearful burns and extended treatments. I had begged for him to be kept at home. How I now regretted that, for at school he would have had regular meals, regular play, schoolmates of his own age, this lonely boy, and been away from the constant nagging of over-keen parents. An ever willing but ailing horse, driven to death.

"Oh God," I cried, "in Thy mercy help me to bear this sorrow, my punishment; I turn to You, my Light of Love, for comfort." As I prayed those words a thought entered my being. 'Have I not shown you there are other Worlds of greater Happiness, than being alive? No death, if you believe in Me.' I got up from my knees, refreshed and comforted, and then remembered the Vision I had seen during Mary's coming. I entered my bedroom. Yes, those were the windows, close together, as I had seen them; my feeling of weariness and death about. John, my son, and not the doctor, was the other man with the hidden face. I had been prepared for this passing, even to the date. Susan's hair had grown to resemble the spritely-eyed child.

My mother's words, "And you will do it even if this does happen?" "Do what?" My book. Write of my vision and show how life is fated for what reason we know not. Christ came and was to die, but if we believe Love will help us and comfort us as no earthly person can.

The comforter

That night when I went to bed and lay down to sleep I saw the moon peeping through a crack in my curtain. Near it was a bright happy star that twinkled brilliantly, and suddenly went out, came again and again disappeared. I felt somehow my son was connected with that star I had never seen before, or would ever see again. I shut my eyes to try and sleep; awoke with a start. A large perfect "soul light" floated before my eyes and out towards the star. It was like those I had seen being blasted as the people on the brink dived into the Light. This one, I knew, had passed the trial and had been large, perfect and unbroken. A voice spoke to me to take courage, bear suffering bravely for this is your son's soul; he has won glory and happiness. I turned over and thanked my God, and slept.

I always prayed at night and in the morning, looked in the daily paper at the Personal Column for my answers. Next morning the first letter to be opened was from a much loved sister-in-law by marriage. She had enclosed a text for 31st March; the day of John's passing – Sunday. "Believe in God and immortality' … There is no death in the world except forgetfulness. Everything that loves, and has loved to death, meets again". Mazzini. And picking up my daily paper I read: "The Spirit Himself beareth witness ... that we are children of God ... heirs of God and joint-heirs with Christ. Romans VIII 16-17."

The second day I read from the paper: "Our Saviour Jesus Christ ... gave Himself for us, that He might redeem us from all iniquity, and purify unto Himself a peculiar people. Titus XI 14."

On John's third day, when 'the soul shall rise again', I read: "An entrance shall be ministered unto you abundantly into everlasting Kingdom of our Lord and Saviour Jesus Christ. II Peter I 11."

The day of John's burial: "The Holy Spirit ... He shall teach you all things, and bring all things to your remembrance, whatsoever I have said unto you. St. John XIV 26."

Then I prayed earnestly if it was time for me to write my book. The answer: – "The word is very nigh thee, in thy mouth, and in thy heart, that thou mayest do it. Deuteronomy XXX 14."

All these were from *The Daily Telegraph* personal column.

In the evening, when it had been time for his return home from work, I looked towards the setting sun and prayed for him. One evening at this hour I was wandering down the garden path, my back to the sunset. The Reveille sounded from the Boys' Home nearby. A rushing wind seemed to race down the path after me. I felt a caress. My eyes filled with tears as I murmured "John". The wind raced on. I remembered it was the evening of his third day.

During that week the weather turned cold and wet. My house was filled with butterflies; the butterflies he had collected and loved so much as a boy, Red Admirals, and tortoise-shell peacocks, he had called them. I thought of his description of death to little Mary – like caterpillars, to rest as a chrysalis and wake again as a butterfly. Some days after the funeral the sun shone again and I was out, digging amongst the flowers. A Red Admiral came and settled on a flower nearby. "John," I spoke aloud, "are you enjoying a larger, happier life now, like that butterfly?" The butterfly arose, fluttered against my cheek, a soft caress, and then up, up, it went, straight up into the sun, and dazzled out of view.

Many days later – John's Whitsuntide – I woke one early morning to see him enter my room, dressed neatly in his navy blue suit. He came straight towards me, and sat at the foot of my bed. "Mother," he said, "give up mourning, for I am perfectly happy. I have come to tell you so." I sat up in bed, and stared at him hard. How well he looked. He vanished. Suddenly all the birds seemed to have awakened to sing their morning song of glory to God. I woke my husband, and told him. "I have seen John. He is happy."

And every night small Mary prayed aloud at her mother's knee, saying at the end of her mother's dictated prayer, her own small prayer: "And please God give brother John a happy time with you. Amen."

Extracts of letters

My mother gave more: these are a selected few.

From the sister-in-law staying with them at the time:
I feel I can never forgive myself for running away and leaving you both alone in your sorrow and grief, but I was so unhinged by the tragic occurrence that I felt I would only be a nuisance to you and not a help, as I could not control my emotions like you two brave souls, so I thought it better I should quit. I am sorry, my dears, I failed you, but I felt also I might get ill and cause more worry.

Poor dear John, he was a fine fellow and so unselfish; always doing for others and never complaining. You will miss him terribly. It is so terrible to think of him being cut off in his youth, he was so happy in his home and with you all. At any rate the babies will comfort you and you are not left desolate...

I also could not have borne to see his funeral and should have asked you to excuse me. I was so very fond of him and he was always very sweet to me.

From a Doctor who knew John and saw his burns:
We read in the paper yesterday of the death of poor John. I am quite sure myself that the acute cardiac dilation was due to 'histamine' poisoning of his heart muscle, the result of his burns. Don't blame yourself for it; these acute cardiac dilations are the devil. ... You must not blame yourself, what you did was for the best; no one could have foreseen this. It may comfort you to know that a burned leg like John had, sometimes the poison lies dormant and does not come out, and then this happens, but no one is to know it is so.

To the Father:
As one who served under you I wish to offer my deepest sympathy in your sad bereavement. I have always considered it an honour to have served under you as the fairest and squarest C.O. an airman can have. I never knew your son but can imagine a kind of young lad he must have been.

From a stranger:
If you remember I was 'warded' in 'Ashley Cooper' in Guy's about a fortnight after John was admitted and in no time we became very firm friends. I realised the pain he was suffering then and I admired him tremendously for the cheerful spirit he maintained throughout. It is no exaggeration to say that he was 'the life and soul' of the ward. We used to fight, argue, play hockey with brooms on the balcony and spend hours doing our daily bit to help the nursing staff and no time during those eight long weeks we were together did anyone even hear the slightest murmur of discontent from John. Truly a severe test for a man's character, let alone a boy's. Most people in the ward were known by their bed number, but it was ever 'No. 21', always 'John'.

From a new Headmaster:
I knew John four years ago when I was, for one year, vice-master, and had a deep affection for him. I left before his serious accident. He had a most attractive and loveable disposition. The school was going through a difficult period of transition at that time, and I always felt that John kept himself unspotted in not altogether easy circumstances, though he had all the high spirits and mischief proper to a boy of his age.

From a school matron:
I must write to tell you how shocked I was to see the most tragic notice of John's death. He was such a dear boy when I knew him years ago, and I still think of him when I used to try and amuse him when he was not well. ... Dear John! There was something quite different about him to other boys. He was so thoughtful and rather old-world; it is indeed sad that such a promising young life should go like that; at least so it seems, but then one does not know.

From the man who offered to take the lad into his office:
I know of no way of adequately conveying to you both my very real sympathy. Possibly the shock was severe to even myself because I, as I so often told you, had not only a definite liking for John, but a great belief in him also. I know no boy of his age for whom I had a more genuine regard – but "those whom the gods love ...."

From some-one who knew him in Egypt:
I was terribly grieved to see that you have lost John, that very cheery boy who I so well remember at Aboukir – so full of beans at all times. *(One of two similar remembrances of him at Aboukir.)*

Cause of Death according to the findings of the Doctor:

My mother gives the whole report; his summary was as follows:

SUMMARIZING the POST MORTEM findings:-

There was acute dilation of the chambers of the right side of the heart, they dilated and became distended with blood that was drawn into them by each respiration. Becoming over stretched and distended they were unable to contract and consequently circulation ceased. As a result of this, fluid was poured into the lungs and produced the condition I have described to you.

There can be no doubt that the run was the actual causative factor that was responsible for the dilating of the chambers of the right side of the heart, and it is important to remember that the same thing happened, to a lesser degree, only a few weeks ago. But exertion like this could not cause a fatal result in a perfectly healthy heart, it could only result in a flabby heart, such as was found in this case, whose chambers can over distend on exertion beyond the point of contracting again and performing their function.

There was no organic disease in the heart that would cause the condition, but certain poisons circulating in the blood can render the heart very liable to dilate dangerously on exertion. The commonest poisons to do this are the poisons of Rheumatic Fever, Scarlet Fever, Influenza and Septic Poisoning. The extent to which Influenza can occasionally affect a heart seems to bear no relation to the severity of the attack, and I think it extremely probable that the severe cold associated with a temperature that the deceased suffered in December last, was an influenza attack, and this belief is, to some extent, strengthened by the statement that has been made that this cold recurred in January and March, and he still had some slight bronchial catarrh at the time of his death; recurrent attacks seem to be a feature of this year's epidemic. Also I think there is further confirmation evidence in the fact that since Christmas the Deceased had not been well. Influenza is sometimes more easily diagnosed by its prolonged convalescence than by its mode of onset.

Finally the septic absorption from the abscess under his tooth may have had some added effect on the general situation, and I think that the unusual and prolonged effect on the boy of a tooth extraction is also significant of latent trouble.

The cause of death was asphyxia due to the flooding of the lungs with fluid after the circulation had ceased.

I give the cause of death then as:-

(1) Acute Oedema of the Lung due to
(2) Acute Dilation of the Heart the result of
(3) Influenza.

PART IV

TRANSFORMATION

My mother wrote a Part IV circa 1956-7 on her life after John's death. My summary shows her transformation from submissive wife to a modern woman, capable of realising her potential and earning a living. My own memories being limited, I also make use of research on my father's life by Philip Cracknell – http://battleforhongkong.blogspot.co.uk/2014/09/wing-commander-alfred-horace-steel.html. I end with her own summary of where she had arrived in 1960 in her understanding of God's love, after much anguish caused by the love for her husband that refused to die.

The growth of self-confidence

My father and mother diverged mentally after John's death. My mother found some consolation in her knowledge that he was with the everlasting Love. My father rejected a god who could take away his son, and no longer felt he need obey the seventh commandment: Thou shalt not commit adultery. His career had reached a successful point: Cracknell reports that he was Regional Inspector for London and Middlesex Air Raid Precautions. He could no longer bear to drive himself after the dreadful trip to fetch his dying son. He went by train to the office but my mother drove him when he had meetings and talks elsewhere. They could now afford a resident mother's help for their two young daughters. She made a point of returning to fetch him in time to hear his last lecture, learning much about the subject, and thus became able to help him in seeing how things might affect women.

In 1937 my father was sent to Hungary to attend a realistic demonstration of a bomb raid there. He was given a diplomatic passport for the purpose. He used it to bring back a pretty, young Hungarian girl. Money for my mother became very short again. She accepted an invitation from her mother-in-law to stay in rooms she took for them by the sea. After a time her mother-in-law arranged for my father to be invited down to give a talk locally and set the scene up for a reconciliation. The Hungarian girl vanished.

Soon afterwards my father was offered a post in Hong Kong, to start up Air Raid Precautions there. They were both glad to leave the house with its sad memories. We sailed for Hong Kong on 11th February 1938, arriving there six weeks later. Initially he had only a shorthand typist to help him. My mother joined some policemen in taking an examination to qualify her for teaching ARP and was given an office alongside his to recruit and train women wardens who came to number over 1,000. In June 1940 the government ordered the evacuation of European women and children to Australia in view of the Japanese advance down the coast of China. Some women refused to go and some were exempted because of their work, but my father, who was put in charge of the evacuation, insisted on us departing.

While we were in Australia, he acquired a Chinese mistress, Mimi Lau, who worked for one of the companies supplying equipment to the ARP, to whom he gave costly gifts. When queries arose over the payments made to contractors for the building of tunnels and other air raid shelters, there was an official enquiry, running from August to November 1941. Hong Kong papers gave his affair with Mimi Lau much publicity (though the news did not reach Australia). Cracknell writes that the enquiry cleared my father of any financial misdoing but the report was not published, being overtaken by the Japanese siege of Hong Kong. His secretary, who is still alive, remembers him as a good employer, of whose financial probity she was convinced.

My father was transferred in December 1941 to India as Adviser on Civil Defence and sent for us. After a year in Delhi, he made Shillong, a hill station in Assam, his headquarters as it was evident that the main need for his work was on the borders of Burma. He was with us sporadically when snatching a few days of leave. Meantime, my mother ran canteens for the troops who came to Shillong for brief respites from the jungle warfare in Burma. At the end of the war she received grateful thanks from the officers commanding them for making these a social area where the men could relax in as good conditions as were possible in temporary encampments. She also took into our house children from the tea plantations in the plains, who came to Shillong for schooling. Every house in Shillong was required to be fully occupied in the wartime emergency. The boarders gave her some income independent of her husband; all her other work was on a voluntary basis as a member of the WVS (Women's Voluntary Service). Socially she was on friendly terms with the wives of the Generals engaged in the Burma campaign; Una Slim was one of my class-mates.

When the war with Japan ended on August 16th 1945 my mother was asked to go to Hong Kong to help with the repatriation of internees there, as she had been advertising for and keeping a record of the addresses and movements of the relatives of Indians and other nationals who had been interned by the Japanese during the occupation. My father also wanted to return to Hong Kong and gave his permission for her to go. However, to his wrath, he was told to stay in Burma to assist in the repatriation of civilian internees there, having being made a temporary Lt. Colonel for this purpose. (My mother was going as part of the unpaid WVS.) She left in early September and, after some difficulties solved by her high-up contacts, reached Hong Kong. Here she was blasted with the story of Mimi Lau. When her duties were over, in late November, she telegraphed me to come with my sister to meet her in Calcutta. We were met at Calcutta station by my father, who by chance had also finished his duties, and who had just been told by his niece that we would be on the afternoon train. My mother's ship arrived soon after.

Their meeting was not happy. The outcome was that on December 22nd we flew back to England, having a medical priority. (I had broken my elbow soon after she left Shillong, where the nature of the injury had been misunderstood. By December the elbow's immobility required an immediate operation by a skilled surgeon.) My father stayed, initially saying he would follow us. He did not, having developed another relationship in Burma, which was to result in a son, given the name Christopher, in 1947. He went into business there and initially did well enough to pay our school fees and to give my mother a sporadic allowance which averaged about £200 p.a., more than she had ever had before, but still not enough for a middle-class life in post-war Britain.

At fifty-one my mother had to begin to earn a living. Borrowing money from one of his relatives, she took a half share in a riverside café in Buckfastleigh, Devon. My sister and I waitressed in the holidays. The freezing winter of 1946-7 led to a broken back when she fell from a ladder after checking the water tank in the loft. She returned to work in plaster, promising coaching companies a free meal for their driver if they stopped off there. With its rising turnover and the improvements she had made (such as finding a water supply other than the River Dart), she was able to sell the business on advantageous terms and to invest in a guesthouse and restaurant in a village nearer our school. This did well in the summer and at Christmas; there were difficult times in between. Meanwhile, she was being stressed by her husband's requests for divorce. He would not provide the solid evidence of adultery with a specific woman, then needful for an English divorce, saying only that he had had many women, a statement my mother found extremely hurtful. Her trusted solicitor strongly advised her not to agree to his suggestion of a Burmese divorce.

In November 1949, when I was in my first term at Cambridge, my father telegraphed that he was returning in early December. We did not immediately realise that Burma had been engulfed in a civil war a year after independence in 1948 and that he had lost everything in the disorder, except for his RAF pension. Shortly after arrival he summoned me to come by myself to meet him. I did not enjoy having to return to tell my mother that he did not wish to see her ever again. I coped with the stress by learning to put my parents' problems into the framework of my life; something that had to be accepted and dealt with as necessary, but which need not affect the picture I was drawing in the centre. This has had the effect that I do not remember the details of any of my meetings with him except the first. My mother was naturally even more stressed, suffering migraines and other psychosomatic troubles while still continuing to run her business.

Their first meeting was in Exeter some five months later, probably in early May 1950. It was arranged by his eldest brother's wife. My mother prayed earnestly for guidance. Her trusted solicitor had retired and it was his son who was taking her to the meeting. In the morning she read "and to godliness, brotherly kindness; and to brotherly kindness, charity", 2nd Peter 1.7. At it, she learnt for the first time that my father had a three year-old son. He said he was very worried as he did not know where he was. His mother had left him to return with her four other children to her husband. A divorce was no longer necessary. Appalled by the thought of a deserted waif in Burma, my mother told my father to bring him to England, legally adopt him and care for him himself. He was looking so ill and shattered that she felt he must have someone to live for. It was arranged that he would call at the hotel, see his daughters and that with their agreement, his life insurance, taken out at their marriage and legally for the benefit of his wife and children, would be cashed in and used in part to fund flights to Burma to recover the child. Driving her back, the young solicitor warned her against this, but she was determined.

Returning later to thank her sister-in-law, she was shown a picture of a handsome Burmese woman. My mother exclaimed that she was not the one whose photo her solicitor had received when they were discussing divorce. (Chris's mother had a British father and a Burmese mother.) She went to his office to check. It was clearly another woman. Was the second woman the real reason why he wanted to go back to Burma? My father apparently acknowledged this new love when she challenged him.

Nevertheless the meeting about his life insurance went ahead. Apparently I took minutes of their agreement on how the money was to be divided up, roughly equally between them, and then got them to sign each page as a true record. They both had uses for it but not for the air flights which justified my father's share. Family evidence shows that Chris was already in England. He had come home with our father and both were taken in by his elder sister Edie, then aged seventy-five, who looked after the small boy till she died in 1955.

My mother's feelings towards her husband were often bitter but even as a young woman I could recognise that this was the flip side of a coin which still had love engraved on its reverse. Some subsequent meetings were hostile, as when he came to the hotel to demand money. A doctor writing of her migraines in 1953 observed that "her husband still continues to badger her for money and she still shells out". Others were amicable, arranged at his request. Apparently she always took either me or Susan with her as she did not trust herself. In March 1956 he dined us all well to discuss his worries about Chris's ability to pass an exam necessary to get him into Christ's Hospital, a charitable boarding school with which a friend of his was connected. (I apparently gave sage advice, as a teacher myself then.) It seems that soon after he suggested a reunion. She says her heart was willing but, remembering his "many women", in concern for her daughters, she wrote asking about his medical fitness, implying, though not stating, her fear that he might have contracted a sexual disease. His bitter wrath ended the matter.

Superficially, she took this smoothly. She did voluntary work for the WVS again. She took an active interest in the local United Nations Society, organising their house to house collection for Hungarian refugees in 1956, and becoming its secretary later. She went back to her book, rewriting it in the third person version, as I had suggested to protect privacy, and tried to get it published, either in a version that ended with John's death or, if my father agreed, with an added section, Part IV, on her life afterwards. Publishers found it too personal as did the Rev. John D. Pearce Higgins, who wrote to her on receipt of her story, in December 1959. He had knowledge of psychology, using this to test the validity of such accounts. He accepted her story as true, and enclosed one of his parish magazines in which he had published two touching Victorian experiences on the same lines. He recommended sending it to the Churches Fellowship for Psychical Study. She did so immediately, again without success.

However, revisiting her Vision when she had failed to take him back had in fact plunged her into inner conflict and despair. While working on this book I found some typed pages on the understanding of her Vision at which she had arrived, with a handwritten addition on a final lone visit to my father, which finally restored her peace.

God and the universe

For us to see how we have to fit in God's jigsaw puzzle of the Universe, to become something greater than we are on this earth, we have to study both worlds as one 'whole', and to realise that life here on this earth is a kind of Fate, a part we have to play which will only by our own endeavour get us back to a still greater place in the "After Life".

Christ was warned in Heaven before he undertook to go through the same circle of life as we are asked to do. He knew the tragic end of this earthly Life that He had to face, but because He also knew and remembered His Heavenly Father – His Parent Light, the Light of Godhead, that he was part of, He wished to prove to us that it was worthwhile to suffer here on Earth ... whether by mind or body. The way we tackle that problem so as to improve our characters is what is needed from us and counted, by our own endeavour, freedom and will power. If we make ourselves in a fearful muddle of mind there are men of stronger understanding, such as His Disciples, to help us over our problems. There are many disciples to help us still in this present world, godly men and women who can help untangle our muddled minds. ... I am prepared for men of greater science to peer into, and try to find from my book a path to greater understanding of this our Universe. There are sure to be many ready to scoff and ridicule, and especially in one's own family, to exclaim "How you exaggerate," or "Your imagination". Yet this inward knowledge given to a few has lead me to persevere and to find out and use the wonders of what we call Science. These things have ever been with us, but it needed men without fear of ridicule to bring to our knowledge and daily use the telephone, electricity, wireless, television, the atom and the power of the "H" bomb and still more to come. The Devil has power over this world as well as God.

Up to the word 'atom' her typed pages follow a manuscript most probably written early in 1957, as they are on the back of duplicated sheets of the March-July 1957 programme of the Enfield branch of the UNA. That manuscript continues with reflections on her earlier vision and John's death. The typed pages I recently found probably date from late 1959. They add the H Bomb to the list and continue as shown below. The British test of its own H bomb was carried out on May 15th, 1957 and launched a national debate about the rights and wrongs of having such a weapon.

To whom are we giving ourselves? "Our Father which art in Heaven, hallowed be thy name, on earth as it is in Heaven" should be the daily, nay hourly prayer of those who wish for God to win through. For the conflict is on, in our midst. With the "H" bomb we have reached a point, a freedom to decide our Fate. God or Devil. Who do we will to win?

The New Testament and Old have references to this "on earth as in Heaven" and the coming and going of souls between this earth and Heaven, such as Jacob's vision in the Old, and other references in the New Testament, including in "Revelations". Perhaps, after all these years of human earthly struggle over good and evil, the Maker of All Things may feel we have reached a development to be allowed to know more. We learn of the fearful destruction and evils of these new sciences and then we learn how to control them, as one feels God does and has done all these years. These things new to us have always been within our orbit. Perhaps the physical make up of our children is to be changed and they will be able to travel further into the knowledge of the spiritual as well as into space while on this earth. To me it seems the present day youth wishes not only for more freedom than we did, but an outlet for his or her energy. They really do think more deeply. They have so much more to learn. They need this freedom. We must have faith in our help for them and trust them when they wish to stand on their own feet. If we believe in God and remember God is Love, we will have Faith and Hope in the good we have tried to live ourselves winning through in them.

"Time" never stands still. Why should our Maker?

Failures, freedom, despair and peace

Looking back on my life, rereading what I had written twenty five years ago of my first vision … I reflected my boy had died while still a minor, and still under our complete care. He had achieved what he was sent out to do. The way he bravely bore his sufferings and chidings proved this. He may not have succeeded in his earthly advancement, but he did in his spiritual character, which is the advancement we need for a life more eternal than this one of death is. That is what is asked of us, to increase the power of the good Light. All light has to be fed.

Standing on the Brink I had that wonderful feeling that God was Love as well as Light. Yet I failed to understand what I should do over this bitterness my husband was now showing towards me, according to my daughters and other relations, and which he could write but never say when we met. He would ask to see me privately and I was glad to go, but I felt I could not trust him blindly as I used to do. I would take a daughter and calm myself for my attitude by saying he would be pleased to see her. Her presence spoilt the freedom of speech for both of us. If I had gone alone I should have proved my trust both in God and in him. But I always failed. I could not go alone.

I had the power to trust God for my "Daily Bread". I would pray for advice and do whatever I felt I was told by it to do. That might be contrary to a solicitor's advice and yet I would win, and found I had done the right thing. My life was very different to the days when I had to do as my husband wished. I loved to stand on my own feet. I enjoyed my freedom. No chiding. When I had made an error I could sit back and quietly think how to get over it, with no inferiority complex to overcome. It added more fun and thought to life. I had more time for the joys of the children. I had more money to spend and could do what I wished with it. The longer he stayed away the more difficult was it for me to go to him when he asked me. So I failed to go, and wrote to him asking after his health instead. My Spirit rebelled against me. I fought it, crying out I would rather become dust, a nothing any more, and wept most unhappily at my own weakness and fears. Ten years ago I was anxious to forgive and to give, but I had only received rebuffs, and now I was tired and old, wanting only peace. No people. Only the birds, flowers and a faithful loving dog. *[She had in the late 1950s acquired a miniature poodle.]* No more chiding.

Yet the knowledge that we cannot just become dust, otherwise why would Christ have suffered so much? So I reasoned we must forgive and love. Because I had lost my opportunity by that letter, it so upset me that I became really ill. My head ached, my ears buzzed. I used to fall suddenly, generally when out, getting great cuts and bruises. No Doctor or specialist could explain the reason. *[Tests of hearing, reactions, blood pressure, eyesight were all normal or better than average.]* It was just this mental worry. That was what my Mother feared would happen – hence her voice appealing to the Light to explain to me "forgiveness of sins" and other matters. It was the knowledge of my hardness that made me so ill.

It is also why it has taken me so long to finish this book. I had told myself it was because I did not wish to hurt my husband's feelings or that of his family ... *[After more than a year's delay a letter from his solicitors dated 11th May 1958 told her he refused permission to publish her book. In 1959 she obviously felt this was because of the last section, and was now submitting the version with disguised names, but ending with John's death.]* Now it goes to a publisher of Christian literature which God put unexpectedly in my path at the church where I worship. That it must be published comes to me from verses out of my daily newspaper and a hymn that we were sent home with after being told to help this Society. *[This society in fact provided literature to African churches, but seems to have passed it on to the Rev. John D. Pearce Higgins, whose letter of 22nd December 1959 was mentioned earlier, for in ink* "Now it goes" *is crossed out and* "It went" *substituted. She then adds, in ink, an addition which she indicates should have gone before this last paragraph:]*

While staying with a sister-in-law I heard that my husband had been ill and in hospital, but was out again. I made up my mind to go and see him. My own "ulcers" having been very upsetting to me, I wrote warning him of my coming, giving my phone number and permission to reverse the charges. Off I set as I had had no reply from him. I found him in a dear wee detached house, with a caravan in the garden, for his son's playroom. A car and a large glass-house. He opened the door, surprised but pleased. Then a younger woman's voice and he refused to allow me to come in. *[She is at the bottom of the page and squeezes in more notes.]* His house-keeper. He would have much to give up. The curtains. Front door and his appearance looked so well kept. I was glad. My ulcers healed. He was happy and fine-looking in his old age. I returned home to publish my book.

Chris, my half-brother, says this was the house of the Rendalls, a childless couple who were good friends of my father and Edie. My father must have given my mother this address to keep his own secret. Chris loved Mrs Rendall, who often took him out, and he lived with them after our father died, their caravan becoming his bedroom. Hers was probably the voice my mother heard. After Edie died Chris remembers he and his father living in one room in a series of tatty boarding houses, until a widow provided greater comfort and two rooms. My father's poverty was genuine; the occasional splurges may have been due to betting wins.

However, his last deception gave my mother peace. She had made the effort to go alone, ready to fan up the embers of their love if he wanted it; she had found he did not need her and neither, apparently, was he in need. She could now put their love in the past where it belonged, ready to enjoy the new kinds of love that the future offered. In February 1960 I met the man who was to become my husband. We married in August. My father gave me £100 for the costs of the reception and came to the wedding, so both my parents were there. In May 1963 I took his eight-month-old grandson to see him. He was by then in a nursing home. He died on 27th December that year. By then my sister was also married. My mother became a loving, happy and active granny to both our children. As my husband's work soon involved being abroad, she paid winter visits to us in Nigeria and Malawi, adding on trips elsewhere on her way home. She enjoyed seeing new places as much as in earlier days, until a time when long flights became inadvisable.

She continued to look out for opportunities to publish. A 1967 refusal from Gollancz was complimentary "It is a very touching document and it is rare to find a true revelation written about in such a sincere and straightforward manner. The problem is principally that the story is too personal for general publication ..." Her last known attempt to get publication was in 1974. She died in 1981.

I hope the time is now ripe for her story. I think she will be glad to have it out as a modern EBook as well as in print form!

Lightning Source UK Ltd.
Milton Keynes UK
UKOW01f1543280817
308066UK00003B/52/P